THE

POWER OF INVENTORY

How to simplify, course correct, and use inventory as a strategic advantage

An inventory management, strategy, and optimization playbook

Dustin Offersen

After 15 years of business leadership, analysis, and strategic consulting, I found broad business knowledge innovation to be just as important as the individual products, processes, or systems. I also noted that inventory was always at the source of its success or failure. It is like an electrical phenomenon, similar to emitting light or creating a positive charge, by understanding the impact on inventory one can influence the surroundings and drive change across the business. Like the source of electricity, inventory strategy can build and render extremely powerful results creating a vast influence but can also have catastrophic results if not properly controlled and respected with the right level of maturity.

Thank you to all of my mentors and to my family who encouraged and pushed me along the way. For those that doubted or challenged my ability to succeed, thank you for the humbling extra push. Not everything is easy but anything can be accomplished.

A very special thank you to Lisa for being my rock and partner in everything I do, to Ryan for his "silent" guidance and push all my life, and to Mark for his passion and artistic creativity.

To Chelsea, Courtney, and Garrett who inspire me to be the best I can be... reach for the stars. I know you can make it!

-Dustin

CONTENTS

Chapter 4

Chapter 5

Chapter 6

Chapter 7

The Inventory Paradigm Shift

CHAPTER 1
DEFINING SUCCESS IN STRATEGY AND MANAGEMENT

Inventory Management is more than a passive reporting capability. It is arguably one of the most underutilized and overlooked strategic advantages in a supply chain. Best of all it is a competitive advantage that nearly any company can attain. As company leaders dig deep into their inventory management it is not uncommon for them to find that their inventory team often consists of a siloed and powerless reporting entity that focuses on financial reporting. These teams usually do not have close ties to broader teams, leadership or membership on cross functional teams, or any influence on strategies tied to logistics, procurement, manufacturing, or R&D - however inventories are impacted directly by all of these decisions. Worse yet they may find that any type of inventory planning or strategy is being driven by network, production, or S&OP planning and not even by their own inventory department. As a result they find that an inventory paradigm shift is necessary although difficult to prioritize due to the vast uncertainty of how to accomplish such a task. What should the inventory strategy be to make such a paradigm shift?

Often inventory strategies will fight between two concepts; the first with the intent to abolish inventory and the second to use it as a security blanket. At times, Leaders will try to attain both but needless to say these options rarely ever deliver the intended value and thus do not succeed. As a result they usually come with unintended consequences that take longer to repair than the program took to build. Since commonly there are gaps in how companies truly understand and manage the end to end inter-dependencies of inventory, these broad and simplistic strategies remain unattainable.

Enterprise Inventory Optimization (EIO) programs sell a concept of an end to end vision that optimizes inventory at all levels. What about just implementing inventory optimization as a strategy? Inventory Optimization is one of many trending concepts thrown around the corporate world but most often companies really do not fully understand what it is or the basis behind it. Often EIO is thought of as a safety stock tool by both the company and the software solution team. Unfortunately, a safety stock strategy will not result in the aspired change. A much more complex and broader solution is required to achieve even a simple optimization program. While safety stock is a very tangible piece, it is only a singular part that cannot stand on its own. It is a small part in an overarching process and business need that most companies face.

The majority of inventory optimization programs are just lip service where the company is either exploring implementation, using it as an academic exercise and unable to implement into the real world, or has partially implemented a single step with suppressed results. This is because the academic solutions sold by the software companies often miss the mark on all the interdependencies of a working supply chain. They overzealously assume that the maturity of the current supply chain has the data and accuracy necessary as well as the talent that can handle these complexities seamlessly.

This is not what is intended by leadership. As leadership digs, they find out the maturity and change management of their people and processes are not nearly as mature as they need. As a result, the software solution has limited success. Since the team is held accountable to attain a return investment they piece together what they can and report positive progress.

What would a leading edge company be without a robust supply chain? Bankrupt.

The technical expertise to manage and move the product being sold to meet consumer's expectations is worth as much as the business case and concept. If customer service did not exceed competitors (who likely could instantly meet customers' demands) the company would not succeed no matter how competitive their product. NOTE: Leading companies still struggle with this as leaders spend billions trying to achieve an "instantaneous" response in order to further compete with more traditional styles.

Companies that can implement and master the new technological solutions quickly become best in class in their industry and often see handsome gains in stock prices.

Becoming leaders in the area is not easy. It takes driving internal and external change management with a passion, relationship building of collaborative networks across multiple industries, and strong influence and collaboration with software suppliers. The ability to influence and collaborate with software suppliers is commonly disregarded but it is extremely important to ensure their commitment is as strong as the companies that are implementing it. The software must have the proper investment and enhancements to support the business needs when it is needed and the software company needs this customer feedback to invest their resources wisely. Without the right relationships, change management, and technological investments, history repeats itself and lip service becomes common. It is noted by all the research and white papers available that the majority of the highly technical planning programs are grossly underutilized within their perspective client companies and ultimately fail in environments where the proper investments in people, process, and technology have not been executed.

Current struggles are not the limitations of technology but the limitations of the people that can implement the latest technological capabilities along with the ability to drive continuous process improvements by leveraging this technology. In order to implement, it takes knowledge different than that of a purely academic approach. The leadership and change management skills to enable success of the program are even more important. A strong understanding of the current challenges being faced and an ability to influence and overcome these barriers are also important. It does take a deep knowledge of the mathematical processes but also a deep and detailed understanding of the physical end to end business process. This combined knowledge and capability are all critical to properly address the right areas and ensure the proper foundational stability. In most cases finding and developing the right talent that has all these capabilities is very difficult. So it is back to lip service for most teams - every company wants to get there but few know how or are able to do so. Like all other game changing strategies, this does not come easy. If it was easy it would already be done and everyone would be doing it.

How does a company take a stance to use its complexity as a competitive advantage rather than a hindrance? Step by step. Whether it is one step at a time or multiple steps at once, strategies have to begin at the start and end at the finish and mature along the way. A "crawl, walk, run" mentality should be considered. A company needs to know where they are really crawling and needs to focus on development and where they are more mature and therefore can move quickly.

Many texts speak to following the maturity curve and this could be one of them. Every great company with an equally great strategy has had to take risks and make tradeoffs. The greatest will make them in an educated fashion ensuring that maturity and expectations are the right fit to foster success and growth. Leadership must hold all the pieces to the puzzle and strategically share pieces while empowering collaborative teams to drive towards this success. Leaders of great success stories often ensure there is a clear and concise roadmap for which their team can maintain a passion for.

That is no easy task and how can the topic of EIO do all of that? In its basic form, it cannot, nor can any other single initiative. As outlined in over two dozen concepts to follow, EIO is much more than a safety stock tool. It is a process of continuous improvement across all inventories that influences and drives true best in class advantages. The best suggestion is to match these strategies (and others) with the biggest gaps found in the company. Then build on the maturity of the area. Often the gaps that are the least mature will be easiest to address and return the greatest benefit.

Just as the intent would be to continuously build the maturity of the process, the same should be done with the talent of an organization. Take advantage of the young and highly motivated talent pool that comes out of schools with degrees that promote graduates to think on their own and think strategically. Mentor them heavily while empowering them to drive and mature these capabilities, this will help them build and develop their career and develop the much needed talent pool. It will not take long for those with passion and great intelligence to become the next generation of leaders. Reap the greatest rewards through matching projects and staffing at the right level of maturity to cover as many of these concepts as possible. Combined with the right strategy this should result in any company being able to move from mediocre to truly a best in class leader.

What does this mean and what is a true inventory strategy? A true inventory strategy is a robust, educated, and well informed set of decisions that drives a roadmap of continuous change and improvement. It is in line with the current maturity of the processes it impacts and clearly defines how to attain the targeted level of maturation. None of this is stress-free but with the right understanding and a simplified approach leaders can drive great value and success across the whole business without the broader company carrying a heavy burden or realizing the extent of change that it has gone through.

The process seems manageable but why do so many inventory projects and strategies fail? It is not uncommon for leaders to choose to concede to seemingly simpler, sub-optional approaches than they originally aspired for as they know they cannot drive the ship alone and without a set direction. A common recognition is that the proper talent that is able to handle this type of change is not in place as the broader team lacks the ability. Those limited members that have the ability are usually stuck in operational activities and unable to mentor and empower to the level necessary to make this type of paradigm shift. Often these leaders either concede to the status quo or look to move on in hopes of being able to implement in a different environment. Why does this happen?

Arguably it was due to the plan. Plans do not need to be paralyzing or take months of work to create. They need to start small and snowball from there with a greater purpose in mind. Plans need to address the maturity of the status quo, provide a clear direction, concise roadmap, and show enhancements to the greater vision through adding value across all functions. They need to drive a passion in the teams and be something they can align to and take ownership of.

Thus the paradigm shift that creates change. Change is not easy. Change is slow. Change is good. All terms that leaders hear time and time again and can struggle with daily. Paradigm shifts always take a heavy level of change management especially when coupled with strategy, optimization, or management. Change takes constant awareness and coddling but it is done most easily in stages. These staged changes are most natural to be "one bite at a time" and parallel to the maturity of the company in a "crawl, walk, run" approach. If a process expects a team to sprint when they have not yet learned the techniques of how to crawl, the process will fail.

Implementing the proper paradigm shift to establish the right inventory management will create a natural momentum that will help the company take further steps through the maturity scale until eventually surpassing all competition and becoming best in class by using inventory as a strategic advantage. So let us dive deeper into steps and processes that are simple and manageable but create immense enterprise value through strategies that focus on making life better enterprise wide. Some of these strategies may be taken directly into action like a playbook while others may need to be tweaked to fit the environment. Ultimately these strategies are not a comprehensive list of the potential solutions and are only examples to get the creative juices flowing.

CHAPTER 2

ENTERPRISE INVENTORY OPTIMIZATION EXPLAINED

Enterprise Inventory Optimization (EIO) is about having the right product in the right place at the right time. Much of a company's profitability relies on how well it can flow its product. This encompasses the management of cycle stocks (day to day inventory used in production), prebuild of cycle stock inventory driven by capacity or level loading, pipeline and logistics stocks, and safety stock tradeoffs to improve flow.

It's all about location, location, location - and of course, tradeoffs. In order to manage inventories, companies often focus in many areas but leave a lot to desire in their simplistic planning approaches. While it is common to do some or all of the planning in basic spread sheets, many companies are aspiring to move to more high tech solutions. The speed and maturity of technology used to be the limiting factor but in more recent years this is no longer the case. Software providers and systems have been around for many decades in this space but older versions were too simplistic in comparison to the exploding complexity found in the nature of the physical businesses and supply chains.

Meanwhile, technology growth was much more rapid in other sectors with much higher levels of maturity. This was enabling explosive expansion and globalization, leaving their supply chains to find manual ways to bridge the gap. The most natural solution was to regress to Excel™ until better systems and solutions could be implemented. Years later many of these temporary solutions have become standard and the supply chain has become an anchor rather than a strategic advantage which limits the potential of these companies.

Inventory and the related strategies come in three main buckets; cycle stocks, pipeline stocks, and safety stocks. These three buckets are usually planned in silos during timeframes when this interaction matters most. This is often due to the structure of the teams and planning tools. Years ago this was necessary due to the complexity and the limitations of technology but those confines have since changed.

Long term planning has considered all three buckets for decades but at a lower level of accuracy and at a higher level with limited details. The expectation is that when planning gets closer to actual need that the planning teams will dial in the needs. As this happens the planning gets fragmented into multiple teams that have limited interaction compared to what they should. They rarely have the capability to provide the proper oversight and management across all three planning functions. When one team has responsibility for more than one of the buckets, often they focus expertise on one and use the other to bridge gaps or as a side exercise.

As technology advanced in the planning areas few companies recognized the need to keep up with advancements and made appropriate changes to their planning organizations. This missed opportunity left fragmented and less efficient planning with limited collaboration between team planning the different areas of inventory. By detailing and comparing the planning buckets, leaders and teams can identify the specific synergies and advantages of combined inventory planning and strategy. Technological solutions are much more robust and able to support these demands and continue to improve. They are able to break down each bucket individually, understand what is being done, what the intended goal of the process is, and what improvements can be made to improve collaboration, interdependencies, and optimization. Then they are able to combine and compare synergies and address process and technological solutions.

CYCLE STOCK PLANNING

Cycle stock planning is the intentional planning of the amounts of inventory necessary to start a production process within the timeframe needed to start a downstream action. It is often incorporated as a part of replenishment and production planning as a peripheral task necessary to complete these manufacturing plans. It relies heavily on assumptions linked to batch sizes, minimum order quantities, standard lead times, and service times.

Far from an optimization, all of these inputs often are static, dictated, or buffered to enable smooth planning and/or alignment with parallel teams. They are usually accepted as is and "understood" to be very difficult, if not impossible, to change. A true leader will look to understand, question, and improve these processes with passion and an appreciation of the value it can drive.

In addition to these inefficiencies, companies can face massive amounts of cycle stocks wrapped into prebuilt inventories held downstream of a future constraint. Constraint planning can requires more science than instinct but too frequently it is all instinct and little to no science.   While prebuilds are an effective way to manage some of the business needs the related waste can easily consume many of effective gains the strategy can produce.   Commonly leaders look at prebuilt inventory as just a cost of doing business as they cannot separate out the exact prebuilt inventories, related costs, or effectiveness of the prebuild or constraint planning. Ineffective prebuild planning also drives increased holding costs, write-off risks, and expedites fees in both manufacturing and logistics.

Improvements can be made by focusing talented team members to process map out the current cycle stock planning, track and trace the flow of product and to identify areas of opportunity.   In parallel a maturity assessment of people, process, and technology will help teams understand where to invest in improvements.   It is likely that one imbalance is causing a drag on the other elements of inventory planning.

PIPELINE STOCK PLANNING

Pipeline planning faces two common areas and destinies. First it is rolled into production planning through prebuilds, batch size, increased lead times, or by default through an ineffectively planned bottleneck. This pipeline inventory sits awaiting capacity of a downstream function, ultimately resulting in waste. When this is done the visibility of this pipeline stock is lost and, more concerning, the impact is also hidden. If any of these other planning strategies make a change it has a direct impact on pipeline and ultimately can lead to unintended consequences from the change. Lack of visibility and understanding are the two biggest reasons for teams to maintain status quo. By empowering these types of actions making a change becomes even more difficult.

Second, pipeline stock is implemented to support transportation needs through manual adjustments to POs or through standard transit lead times. It is common for these standard and rules of thumb to be aspirational or to be buffered. When aspirational, these targets put heavy stress on the logistics network and result in negative budget implications. When buffered, these lead times result in additional waste and tie up cash flow and storage capacities. As the ever-changing logistics environment deviates further from these rules of thumb or standards over time this imbalance results in greater inefficiencies that in turn results in increased expenses.

These imbalances can cause further breakdown as the teams accountable for driving the result and managing the physical inventories rarely have direct input or connection to the planning of such inventories. By first providing insight and visibility to status quo the company can make improvements naturally but ultimately will need to understand the current maturity and drive strategic improvements.

BUFFER STOCK PLANNING

Planning for intentional inventory buffers are a critical part of ensuring inventory optimization. Without proper inventory buffers the risk a supply chain endures would be catastrophic. Some manufacturing companies may believe they can manage without inventory buffers but this response would be misguided. They either have continuous breakdowns in their supply chain resulting in expensive and inefficient countermeasures to react or they have buffers built into their other planning processes, usually in their minimum orders, batch requirements, or in their lead times.

There can be many different types and names for buffer stocks. Companies have intentional and unintentional buffers for many reasons where there are more inventories held than needed for cycle or pipeline needs. In a perfect supply chain, cycle stock and pipeline stock is physically moving at all times. Needless to say perfection is basically impossible to attain, only to aspire towards.

To provide the highest understanding and visibility it is important to allocate the right inventory for the right reason and not to use other "levers" to drive inventory. This will cloud the supply chain judgement, reduce alignment, and slow the change whenever a lever is used for reasons other than intended. In addition software companies have defined levers and customize their uses for specific reasons and cannot be held accountable for implications of misuse.

Safety stock is only one type of buffer but can also incorporate some additional categories of buffer stocks. In an accurate portrayal, "using the right levers for the right reasons", safety stocks are specifically designed for the use of protecting against *measureable* supply and demand variability. This measurement can be from future or historical data and could be for regular or highly intermittent risks.

For regular and historical risks safety stock is operationally necessary to "grease the wheels of day to day actives." When the past is not indicative of the future, actions can be taken to make adjustments to the inputs to drive more accurate results. This is a highly statistical approach to the inventory buffers in order to serve the purpose of operational safety stock needs.

In addition to the operational safety stock needs there is often a strategic need to buffer against low risk, high impact volatility. This need requires an understanding of the strategy of the company and the catastrophic events that may be detrimental. In this case the process for defining the inventory buffer may be different than that used to define operationally necessary safety stocks but should still be statistical and fact based. At times there may be need to proxy data to complete this analysis but this proxy should be factual and representative of the attributes and levels of the actual process it is serving as proxy for. The resulting buffer is a strategic level of safety stock buffer that is implemented to cover for low likelihood but high impact risks.

There are many ways to define safety stocks and even more levels of complexity that can be incorporated in to ensure accuracy. Businesses enact programs from simple rules of thumb to highly sophisticated and expensive Multi Echelon Inventory Optimization Safety Stock Strategies. This is a case where effort equals value. The rules of thumb come with massive costs due to ineffective inventory management. The highly sophisticated and dynamic software approaches are expensive but come with the best return. They usually are difficult to synthesize and sell into the business due to the massive transformation necessary. The journey has to come over time, first identifying the current status and maturity and building upon that until an optimal solution is created.

SINGLE ECHELON SAFETY STOCK PLANNING

Single Echelon Inventory Planning (SEIP) is often thought of as a basic safety stock planning approach. Originating as an academic theory, the *base* algorithm of the program ultimately solves for the inventory necessary to cover for historical supply risks, historical demand risks, and a targeted customer service desired through inventory. Supply chains find the need to expand from the academic concept by adding in for key impacts of the supply chain not taken into consideration. This becomes a necessity as the supply chains start to identify implications of trying to take such a simple academic approach to a complex process. When teams quickly move on to more sophisticated planning approaches they put heavier rigor into the inputs and more detail into their outputs, as such the maturity grows to a real SEIP planning approach.

SINGLE ECHELON INVENTORY PLANNING

As the concept of single echelon planning matures it migrates from a safety stock focus to a broader focus encompassing all inventory drivers of the supply chain. Teams find that the inputs provide more insight and value than the outputs. They focus on breaking down barriers by driving change with intent to improve inputs as an avenue to control outputs and meet inventory targets. Strategy changes from a safety stock driven by historical outcomes to a more proactive approach of identifying drivers of risk and incorporating them into the inventory plans and targets. At this stage they are still planning each echelon, or level, of the supply chain independent of another but they have grown the understanding and maturity of inventory and its role within the supply chain.

MULTI ECHELON SAFETY STOCK PLANNING AND OPTIMIZATION

The next level of the inventory maturity curve then moves towards the need to understand the inter-dependencies of the inventory within the supply chain. Inventory accountability comes along with the increase understanding and visibility making this team more responsive to the impacts inventory has across echelons. When one or more products do not arrive on time for a combined assembly then production is delayed if the proper inventory buffers are not in place. This accountability and awareness creates a new paradigm as inventory begins being integrated into more decisions and accuracy becomes more crucial.

Now enters the concept of multi echelon. Most commonly this concept starts with the understanding of inter-dependent inventory buffers and slowly moves to optimization of these buffers. In specific they start with the safety stocks as they are statistically identifiable. Once the optimization of these safety stocks stabilizes with seemingly subpar results - versus original expectations - teams really start to understand the overall complexity. They dig into what it takes to drive the aspired results and they start to broaden their scope to look at the detailed interdependencies of all inventories.

MULTI ECHELON INVENTORY PLANNING AND OPTIMIZATION

Companies often get caught up with and sold on the dreams of Multi Echelon Inventory Optimization (MEIO) and overlook the maturity required to be able to implement. As outlined above there are many steps and prerequisites before a team can take on implementing such a sophisticated program. Conceptually the software can just be "turned on" but just as any process - it is a 'garbage in, garbage out' environment.

Even in the extremely rare occurrence that the core team is brilliant, properly staffed, and has access to the best possible data, the rest of the company has to be prepared to operate within the constraints and assumptions of the program. Alignment across the company with a clear understanding of what the program results will do is critical. Most programs assume internal supply nodes can endure customer service from their upstream partners as low as 50%. If not, there needs to be an ability to identify and set the right parameters. It also has to assume the inputs are accurate including the active Bill of Material (BOM), costs, demonstrated lead times inputs, properly lagged forecasts linked to point of decision, actual consumer orders (not shipments), and customer service targets. In addition to the basics, the supply chain has to conform to the constraints of the tool or the tool has to be customized to meet the unique constraints of the supply chain. *If anywhere a maturity assessment is necessary - it is before the start of an MEIO implementation.*

CHAPTER 3
GRADING ON A MATURITY CURVE

Understanding the maturity of each area and strategy throughout the company is an important step to creating a paradigm shift. A successful course correction first comes by the understanding what the current maturity and status quo is. Trying to take a process from a level 2 to a level 10 is impossible without hitting a few of the levels in-between on the way. Taking enough time and attention to hit each level on the way will ensure a strong foundation and add the most stability and value to the process.

Throughout the next few chapters it will be important to have a grounded understanding of the current maturity. This includes a clear understanding of the maturity in each area of business and the ability to increase that maturity. Each concept comes with a set of example projects and proposals that will attain the highest likelihood of success if applied in a fashion that is complementary to the current level of maturity and development. Each company and industry may find slight variations to the maturity level definitions in order to address certain criteria. The important part is that there is alignment with the maturity level definitions and that everyone understands the maturity assessment and agrees to the same maturity targets.

LEVEL 1

A level 1 maturity should indicate a basic comprehension in the area but with obvious gaps. As an initial level, often teams will struggle on the day to day and implication of the daily actions cause drain on supporting or parallel functions. Where tools and processes exist, they are chaotic. Any change or issue that is not the normal course of duty is likely to have issue without additional support. The process is unable to operate on its own.

LEVEL 2

A level 2 maturity basic comprehension in the area enables the team to carry out day to day operations with mediocre results. Tools, processes, and systems are archaic but for the most part they exist. Teams seem overworked as they often work harder to bridge the gaps. Without support, the team is unable to handle any change or issue that is not considered normal course of duty and is likely to have issue without additional support. The process is able to operate on its own as long as no issues arise but often still result in extra burden to parallel or downstream teams.

LEVEL 3

Continuing to move forward, a level 3 maturity has moderate comprehension and impacts or risks are able to be seen. Tools, processes, and systems are better and all exist but need vast improvement. It is still an immense amount of effort for the team to absorb change or issues. This will still cause some pressure on parallel or downstream teams. The department is often staffed at a basic level to handle the day to day business with basic talent. The team is unable to make improvement on its own even if desired.

LEVEL 4

One of the more common levels is at level 4. The maturity still reflects moderate comprehension but is mostly autonomous and able to run the process without much support at all. Tools, processes, and systems are able to support the basic needs but need improvement, especially when exceptions or issues arise. The team often has key members that address issues or change. These members often are the interface between other teams and integrate or interpret the needs to the rest of the team. It is most common to find the department "checking the box" and meeting requirements but not looking to do much more. Often, they feel overworked and drained, although some team members feel their knowledge and capability is underutilized.

LEVEL 5

At level 5 maturity starts to show. There is a noticeable difference in comprehension compared to level 4 and a deeper foundational knowledge is instilled across most of the team. The team has some forward thinking but many biases and theoretical understandings remain. Tools, processes, and systems are able to support most needs and the team has created some basic tools to handle exceptions and provide some insight into the near future.

LEVEL 6

Depth should be found across the team at level 6. If key members are lost the rest of the team should be able to quickly absorb the gap and train a replacement. Systems are in check and are fluid with little to no need to manage tools, issues, or exceptions outside the system. Processes are well managed and documented and can be understood by peer entities. The team starts to take on stretch assignments and provides some support to surrounding teams.

LEVEL 7

While not yet considered best in class, at level 7 the team is viewed as a strong entity by its peers internally. It is often recognized by external peers and sources as leaders or experts for a narrow area. At this level there still remain noticeable faults but these faults do not hinder success but limit the upside potential. This team is often recruited to lead or mentor in cross functional environments. This team has a positive persona, demonstrates agility, and demonstrates an open and analytical mindset with little to no visible status quo.

LEVEL 8

At level 8 the team starts to be recognized as an industry leader and terms like "best in class" start to surface. This level of team maturity is heavily symbiotic. It not only has excellent tools and processes, it knows how to strategically leverage these successfully and regularly. It builds and drives paradigm shifts more broadly across peers and other teams and is a nucleus for change management. The team understands the broader implications and the need to be leaders of continuous improvement in order to stay ahead of competition.

LEVEL 9

Maturity beyond level 8 is extremely difficult and nearly impossible for many teams to achieve. It demonstrates the highest capability in the industry and is often reviewed and admired by other industries. Expertise of the group reaches far beyond their responsibilities and the team members recognize this sustained ability is unattainable without a strong peer support and looks to ensure many of its peer groups are at close or similar maturity levels. Competition looks to capitalize on perceived weaknesses and team regularly looks to identify these and strengthen them to develop further competitive advantage. This team is core to the company and often influences or drives strategy for the company.

LEVEL 10

A level 10 maturity changes the foresight and concept of competition. It has truly mastered this capability in such a fashion that they no longer view it as a strategic competitive advantage. Talent development or management is no longer a concern as the self-containing development and mastery is a part of the broad culture. The company now focuses on other capabilities and has little or no worry that competition can exceed its current capabilities. In fact, it would not be uncommon for the company to be willing to share its knowledge and lessons learned widely throughout the industry or even broader.

Level 10 maturities do come with their downfalls as innovation starts to plateau and eventually gets left behind the times. New and hungrier competition has found new avenues to success that exceed the "old" way. As a result, the maturity cycle restarts and the once level 10 maturity is left to chase the new standards of the industry.

CHAPTER 4

UNDERSTANDING THE INVENTORY STATUS QUO

The first step is to truly understand the inventory position of the company. This is more than just a few metrics such as turns and budget. One must look to understand how inventory is managed, who manages the inventory, and what metrics or KPIs are in place. Most of all understand who is accountable, what they know, and if they are in a position of empowerment and control. Take this information to start understanding the current maturity and why the current status quo exists. Do not be afraid to share and socialize this information. This will assist the roadmap process and maturity assessment.

The next question is how this is done. Each step has to be taken in alignment with the current maturity level and roadmap of the company. What it does not have to be is led by senior leadership. These tactics, especially understanding the status quo, can be lead organically from any level or role of the supply chain. In fact it is best to not be initiated from the inventory head or a senior leader. Successful initiatives are commonly delivered by leaders throughout the organization. Leaders are not formed by title but by example, experience, and understanding. A leader driving such an initiative needs to have the knowledge and expertise, or willingness to learn on the fly in order to understand what is truly happening and where improvements can be made. By implementing a few activities a leader can get the ball rolling and provide some inertia. The job then becomes a transformational lead with heavy doses of change management.

The best way to understand the inventory status quo, or any status quo for that matter, is to start to measure it. Start by understanding what metrics exist and how people react to these metrics. Once there is a clear understanding to how people will react to a metric, it can help the leaders and teams better understand the benefits of the metric. It will also help them identify how to manage and influence the outcomes and actions driven by the metric. By starting a few simple initiatives to understand metrics and why they exist, a small team can make a big change without much effort in comparison to the value.

Supply chain metrics drive the central nervous system of a company as it is the broadest and deepest view of what is happening from supplier to customer. First and foremost, look to understand these measurements. By doing so, some simple ideas and projects will become clear. Since potential ideas are not always easy to form and outline, two potential ideas are outlined. Take these ideas and adjust them to fit the needs of the company. Ensure process and end goal are clear to the leaders driving these efforts so that these efforts provide the necessary results to attain the intended goal.

SUPPLY CHAIN METRICS

Best in class supply chain metrics revolve around inventory and if they do not they will not achieve a true best in class status. Inventory is a net result of action. It is a physical, live, and traceable aspect that can identify root causes of an issue. The whole concept of manufacturing and supply chain are to *move inventory* from supplier to customer and add value along the way. The most proactive, effective, and actionable metrics all have inventory ties and foundations. Supply chain metrics that contain a wide variety of proactive metrics and that cover all aspects of supply chain should be the overall goal.

"Quick win" projects:

1. Compile all metrics and KPIs being measured within supply chain. Make these visible to all mid-level leaders within the group and work with them to drive exposure to key team members at all levels within supply chain. Sell the "what's in it for me" or WIIFM by working with key contacts and mentoring them on how and why collaboration benefits them. Find ways to show them how this collaboration will improve their success, their day to day activities, and help them improve their current processes, or try to identify other ways that show why they should collaborate. Find ways to leverage existing metrics more broadly as indicators to change. Compare which are KPIs, informational, and action metrics. Expose and understand the differences - but

make no immediate changes. Intent is to share, socialize, expose, and collaborate within the current state.

> *Theoretical return: Varying ROIs can result but ROI will be high as investment is low and opportunity for success is high.*

2. Review current KPI's and address how they are being understood. Limit the focus to stay within the supply chain organization. This means the KPI must be owned and operated within supply chain. Do not spend much time on impacts outside of supply chain other than acknowledging the impact and documenting it.

Then understand how each team can directly impact the KPI's they are accountable for. If no direct action can be taken to impact the KPI then look to understand the KPI's value. In addition identify what unintended consequences may come from these actions. Take note of consequences that are supply chain specific and look to solve these with future actions and projects.

Finally, look to understand if other measurements that have KPI potential could provide the same results for leadership yet could be directly impacted by individuals or teams and/or reduce or eliminate the unintended consequences without resulting in other negative impacts. Some KPI's that cannot be impacted can still be valued in order to report overall results but ultimately these should be kept to a minimum.

> *Theoretical return: Return varies but ROI will be high as investment is low and opportunity for success is high.*

3. A second level KPI review can be completed once the initial review is complete. Let some time pass post initial review to ensure a demonstrated understanding of what is working and what is not. In other words, is the company able to move the needle with the current metrics and KPIs? Address gaps within KPIs by ramping up the focus and usability of similar metrics or measurements that have potential to replace or enhance the KPI. If no enhancement opportunities exist use this opportunity to create some parallel metrics and start to measure the success of the new processes.

Theoretical return: Return is often incremental but proportional to the initial review and the effort invested.

4. The final quick win will be the most painful but provide the much needed stability. Look to integrate all KPIs and metrics into the same reporting and dashboard capabilities with a global view and future mobile capacity. This should provide the capability to become robust with "real time" visibility. It will need to be integrated into the culture of the business and change with the evolution of the business and culture. There should be no "untouchable" metrics that cannot be reviewed or improved, do not accept legacy reporting unless no improvement can be identified.

Theoretical return: Limited initially but the change in culture is worth every dime.

"Quick Win" Predecessors: Each project is a predecessor of the next. Depending on the attributes and agility of the company additional steps may need to be added between projects to ensure success of the next stage.

"Game Changer" project:

Strategically change metrics and reports to live and actionable metrics. Ensure everyone knows how they can influence and change the results. Make accountability clear and visible, but most importantly timely. Implement software that puts this at the tip of everyone's fingertips and remind them regularly. Develop alerts and processes that drive immediate action and countermeasures. Empower individuals and teams to "act now and explain later." Metrics and KPIs should come from the same data and the same source. Whether reporting to the CEO or to those on the production floor the only difference should be the level they have drilled down to.

> *"Game Changer" predecessors: Strong maturity of current metrics and KPIs along with a clear understanding of how to influence them in a live environment. All quick win concepts should be standard within the culture of metrics.*

Continuous Improvement Environment:

Continuous process to proactively identify changes in the business through these metrics should become a standard. As a result the business can expect a slow but continuous evolution of its KPIs and metrics.

Culture: "Passion to Exceed" and Collaboration

"Process Strategy":

A KPI should have a lifecycle, starting as an informative metric, then a measurement, followed by a metric and finally, once fully vetted, considered as a KPI. Focus at the KPI level needs to be a key component. A list of key KPIs and metrics should be reviewed regularly to ensure the KPIs that drive the best possible business performance are front and center and tied to individual and team performances.

Once the team has the momentum started toward a clearer understanding of supply chain metrics they can then expand the change management by starting to ask similar questions about the broader global manufacturing supply and operations (GMS). The team should not await perfection within global supply chain (GSC) to start conversations with all of GMS. The new momentum and fresh results created at the GSC core will help with the larger team alignment. In reverse the first inceptors found in the broader GMS group will help the core gain further momentum within GSC.

Keep the momentum strong by first working through the change or project within the core supply chain team ahead of a broader GMS team collaboration. By doing so, the team will build the much needed experience to help lead the broader GMS teams through the same journey. There may be a few adaptations necessary for the broader GMS projects but the core concepts will be easier to solidify and adjust in the smaller core of supply chain before trying to add in the supply and manufacturing operations.

GLOBAL OPERATIONS METRICS

Also known as Global Manufacturing and Supply (GMS) Metrics, these are higher level metrics that synthesize manufacturing, financial, supply chain, sales, and external impact metrics to drive higher level strategies and necessary tweaks to future strategies and roadmaps to ensure the company stays best in class. While driven by a few KPIs a supplemental "watch" program of other indicative metrics should always be in place. Inventory remains the key criterion that drives highly effective GMS processes. Ultimately the reason GMS exists is to move and add value to inventory.

"Quick win" projects:

1. Compile all metrics and KPIs being measured throughout the global operations. In this case knowledge is power. Find out how to leverage existing metrics within silos of the organization more broadly. Compare which are KPIs, informational, and action metrics. Expose and understand the differences but make no immediate changes. Intent is to share, socialize, expose, and collaborate within the current state.

    Theoretical return: Varying ROIs can result but ROI will be high as investment is low and opportunity for success is high.

2. Review current KPI's and address how they are being understood. Then understand how each team can directly impact a KPI they are accountable for. In addition identify what unintended consequences may come from these actions. If no direct action can be taken to impact the KPI then look to understand the KPI's value. Recognize if other measurements that could become a KPI could provide the same results for leadership yet could be directly impacted by individuals or teams. Some KPI's that cannot be impacted can still be valued in order to report overall results but ultimately these should be kept to a minimum.

Theoretical return: Return varies but ROI will be high as investment is low and opportunity for success is high.

3.   A second level KPI review can be completed once the initial review is complete. Let some time pass post initial review to ensure a demonstrated understanding of what is working and what is not. In other words, is the company able to move the needle with the current metrics and KPIs? Address gaps within KPIs by ramping up the focus and usability of similar metrics or measurements that have potential to replace or enhance the KPI. If none exist use this opportunity to create some parallel metrics and start to measure the success of the new process.

Theoretical return: Return is often incremental but proportional to the initial review and the effort invested.

4.   The final quick win will be the most painful but provide the much needed stability. Look to integrate all KPIs and metrics into the same reporting and dashboard capabilities with global and mobile capacity. This should be integrated into the culture of the business and change with the evolution of the business and culture. There should be no "untouchable" metrics".

Theoretical return: Limited initially but the change in culture is worth every dime.

"Quick Win" Predecessors: The corresponding project within GSC should be a predecessor of the broader GMS project to ensure the proper growth and maturity. As with GSC, each project is a predecessor of the next. Depending on the attributes and agility of the company additional steps may need to be added between projects to ensure success of the next stage.

"Game Changer" project:

Strategically change metrics and reporting to live and actionable metrics. Ensure everyone knows how they can influence and change the results. Therefore make accountability clear and visible, and most of all timely. Implement software that puts this at the tip of everyone's fingertips and reminds them regularly. Develop alerts and processes that drive immediate action and countermeasures. Empower individuals and teams to "act now and explain later". Metrics and KPIs should come from the same data and the same source. Whether reporting to the CEO to those on the production floor the only difference should be the level they have drilled down to.

> *"Game Changer" predecessors: Strong maturity of current metrics and KPIs along with a clear understanding of how to influence them in a live environment. All quick win concepts should be standard within the culture of metrics.*

Continuous Improvement Environment:

Continuous process to proactively identify changes in the business through these metrics should become a standard. As a result the business can expect a slow but continuous evolution of its KPIs and metrics.

Culture: Bold and Expansive

"Process Strategy":

A KPI should have a lifecycle, starting as an informative metric, then a measurement, followed by a metric and finally, once fully vetted, considered as a KPI. Focus at the KPI level needs to be a key component. A list of key KPIs and metrics should be reviewed regularly to ensure the KPIs that drive the best possible business performance are front and center and tied to individual and team performances.

CHAPTER 5
STRATEGIES TO SIMPLIFY AND COURSE CORRECT

Now that a clearer understanding of the inventory status quo is in progress and leaders have a good grasp on where the company maturity lies, opportunities will begin to arise that provide the ability to start to adjust or course correct. Often much easier said than done, it becomes more about strategically picking projects that start to steer the company towards a transformational goal yet match the current maturity of the company. Too often companies can be a little overzealous with these goals trying to make too big of a step when making a change and ultimately end up fighting the momentum rather than leveraging it.

Everything has mass and velocity so using this inertia to make the change is easier than forcing it in a different direction.

There are many ways to the same goal. Find a path that leads to lower resistance but yet can still get desired change completed in a timely manner.

ROOT CAUSE

Starting with projects that help define and resolve the root cause of waste or ineffectiveness is a key way to start to simplify and course correct. By defining the root cause and pain points teams face can help break down the barriers to change.

Inventory is a net result of action. Ineffective actions drive waste and as a result drive inefficient processes and inventory imbalance. The ability to synthesize and understand what is happening to inventory enables the ability to understand the root cause of an issue, whether that resulted in waste or loss of sales.

"Quick win" projects:

1. Review the new compilation of metrics and look for areas of imbalance. Furthermore review team goals and interview team members to understand their biggest issues. The biggest issues will likely surface quickly so no need to spend too much time. Analyze these to understand what the real root causes are by asking the Six Sigma's 5 Why's, implementing DMAIC (define, measure, analyze, improve, control) process, or any other similar processes. Document all root causes found and socialize this with broader teams to get alignment, no need to attain full buy-in at this stage. Once broader teams align that these root causes are accurate an organic transformation will start. Other leaders

may start to drive some of these newly identified issues on their own. Even if the resolution is not the same as expected, let them drive it as long as they are making positive change.

Theoretical return: Return will be high as these basic concepts are foundational to implementation success of future improvements.

2. Review remaining root causes that have not yet been addressed. Look to understand which have the broadest impact covering many areas, which have the greatest ROI, which would change the least resistance to change, and which are predecessors to others. Balance the prioritization but for the initial quick wins look to match the change with the maturity of the process. Once a few conceptual projects have been identified and align with the criteria above look to lead one or a few projects based on size and complexity. Be strategic and don't look to take on too much too quick. Remember less is more as momentum will be built over time. Also be okay with small incremental changes as the target is a culture of small but continuous change and not a big bang.

Theoretical return: If a strong ROI is not forming, quickly review prioritization and quick wins to ensure they are targeting the current maturity levels. Most often a lack of return is from a misalignment of goals and maturity.

3. Continue to repeat projects on an iterative basis that are identified but be careful to align the maturity and balance the workload. Too often companies start to build momentum and then move too quickly. Leaders end up

suffocating the success by overloading teams trying to meet deadlines or "check the box." Once overloaded, the teams start to lose the passion and focus and start to look for ways to cut corners or meet minimum criteria rather than to really drive for the best results.

> *Theoretical return: Slow but steady will attain the greatest return as long as strategies and teams remain focused and motivated.*

4. Do not overlook the wrap up of the root cause analysis. Once each root cause project has been completed there should be a way to monitor this area for a while to ensure the issue does not reoccur and is actually eliminated. Look to assign a different team to measure and understand the change, this will ensure a better check and balance and longer term success without risk of manipulation.

> *Theoretical return: Limited initially but the change in culture is worth every dime.*

"Quick Win" Predecessors: Mature enough metrics and reporting that enable leaders and teams to identify true root causes. Core teams should be able to facilitate the projects and clearly articulate the value added with supporting metrics as proof.

"Game Changer" project:

There should not be a single game changing project here. What changes the game is the development of the continuous improvement culture. Create true persistence and passion to make change by ensuring clear and visible rewards that have resulted from the change.

"Game Changer" predecessors: No need to await other projects or actions, work to find ways to introduce and ingrain a culture of continuous improvement. It often starts with a positive attitude and a passion for success.

Continuous Improvement Environment:

This review and project cadence of understanding root cause and looking to eliminate inefficiencies should be a sustained and ongoing effort. Use this process to build a culture of looking to continuously increase the maturity of processes throughout the company by looking to identify the root cause of imbalanced inventory. Make sure to allow for and schedule time to do the proper socialization and change management as providing this visibility may be one of the greatest impacts that help the company course correct.

Culture: Persistence and Grit

"Process Strategy":

Start small and manageable. Ensure projects are at the same maturity level as the impacted process. Look to balance cross functional process maturity through considering maturity as a part of the project prioritization. Carefully review the process development. Regularly watch to capitalize on opportunities and look to get others involved to drive changes that impact them.

It is not uncommon to find an imbalance in the maturity of different planning areas that result in a root cause and a need for change. Training is often a large part of some of the easiest changes but often the most under appreciated by the leaders and by the targeted audience. College students spend tens of thousands to hundreds of thousands of dollars to earn degrees that train them on how to think and how to do. Developing mentors and allowing them time to mentor, and support hands on training is one of the most effective and cheapest ways to create change and remove inefficiencies in planning.

This mentorship and training should not only be for new team members but should be a part of everyone's accountability and engrained into the culture. It sounds easier than it is, so how is it done effectively? Again, step by step by managing each area of planning and ensuring the right attention and interaction is given to each area. Leaders should look to allocate some time and empower leaders within their organization not only through providing them the permission to do so but by encouraging and allocating the proper amount of time to deliver such a plan. Look to a few of these ideas as areas to start but do not limit the scope to just these, rather assign resources where the current maturity is the lowest. Attempt to allocate or reallocate resources as necessary to ensure a balanced maturity across all planning functions.

STANDARD LEAD TIME OPTIMIZATION

Standard lead times are the tympani of a supply chain. Just like the tympani drives the passion and heartbeat of an orchestra, standard lead times equally drive whole production and planning process and the effectiveness of Operational Excellence. Too many companies underestimate the importance, often negotiating the settings, or they "set it and forget it," but worst of all they dictate them "thou shalt deliver in 12 weeks." This culture needs to change and they must be set appropriately to enable the supply chain to be successful. Just like in an orchestral piece, timing is everything regarding a supply chain.

"Quick win" projects:

1. Start small by choosing one value stream and looking at the process and flow. Try to "go see" and walk as much of the process as able. If not able, virtually review the end to end process by meeting with subject matter experts and asking them questions. Consider bringing these experts to map out the current process and flows in a face to face event but do not use this as a replacement for walking the process. Do not provide any advice or make any suggestions for change at this time. A part of the change management is showing care and that the team is vested in the process and employees the change intends to impact.

   Theoretical return: No physical return but a much needed part of creating the change that can be easily overlooked.

2. Look to develop processes and ways to measure the demonstrated lead times of the supply chain. Measure this at the most granular level that data is available and roll up from there. This likely will take some system investments and a heavy focus and investment in training and development of key staff that can deliver and validate the process. A good consulting company with the right training and change management skills may be able to support some of the heavy lifting and bridge the talent gap where necessary.

   Theoretical return: Investment will be high but necessary for overall return. This is not a standalone quick win project. This sets the stage to be able to hit the next dozen projects out of the park. Do this right and success is imminent.

3. Planning should be all about getting the right product in the right place just in time without any waste. Ensuring the proper lead times to do so should be the highest priority for a maturing planning process that can understand its capabilities. As outlined, understanding and measuring the demonstrated capabilities are predecessors to this step but now this is where the rubber hits the road and real progress can be made.

   By using the measured capabilities a process can be set up to target a standard lead time update that meets roughly 85% of the time (or any factor generally agreed upon but should be between 1-2 standard deviations). Bear in mind that a corresponding safety stock strategy and production agility must be in place to offset any delays. If confidence and maturity in the processes are low, the team should consider setting the lead times to cover between 90-95% of the deliveries, while a moderate capability can be successful with lead times set to meet 80-90% of the deliveries. If there is a very high level of maturity a team may consider setting lead times to below 80% but should not go below the 70%. Setting shorter lead times can help process throughput and improve the overall efficiency but if lead times are set too low for the current capabilities it will result in more waste and issues than savings. By going below 1 standard deviation results in too many late receipts that inevitably create issues with supply no matter the level of supply chain robustness that is in place. Meanwhile going above 2 standard deviations creates excessive waste and dwell within the supply chain and ultimately has more unintended consequences than added value.

 As a quick win project do this for a single value stream in the supply chain as a proof of value. This will help align and engage the broader organization and develop the motivation to make the change across the enterprise.

> *Theoretical return: This is a big win, incremental gains and efficiencies can be expected throughout. Look for gains not only in supply chain but in sales, manufacturing, and finance (landed costs, cost of goods sold, operating margins, cash flow, and especially inventory).*

4. Watch and adjust to the changes created by project three. If a statistical safety stock strategy is in place recalculate a few months after implementation and put a heavier weighting on recent performance. Measure and watch "on-time" performance in conjunction with downstream inventory buffers. Do not fret or make a change unless downstream impact starts to create bottlenecks or other potentially paralyzing effects. Note that some flux may occur, intent is to understand and balance. If too much occurs, look to revisit and increase the targeted percentage of demonstrated lead times used for the standard. This will be indicative of a process that is less mature than the team originally thought or hoped.

> *Theoretical return: Little to lots, this is the insurance policy. It may cost a lot and have little value if everything runs smoothly. If not, it may prevent total loss and re-secure the project's success.*

"Quick Win" Predecessors: A developing maturity in metrics will be important to enable the necessary support, visibility, and understanding to carry this out. The foundations of root cause abilities will help key in to critical areas of focus and ensure proactive adjustments where necessary.

"Game Changer" project:

The ability to demonstrate success in a single area will help a viral expansion of the standard lead time optimization across the enterprise. The ability to expand this enterprise wide will shift the status quo and be a key course correction.

"Game Changer" predecessors: A successful and mature standard lead time optimization across a single value stream.

Continuous Improvement Environment:

Standard lead times are the heartbeat of planning so having a health check in place as a part of the continuous review and update is a necessity. This does not mean that standard lead times should be changed every time there is a review or even for every change in demonstrated lead times. The culture of continuous review should ensure that the lead times stay in check but with a level of tolerance for change. This tolerance will naturally align as the team defines and maintains the process.

Using root-cause procedures, the team will be able to sense when a misalignment between standard and demonstrated is starting to cause issue and where a change will be beneficial. Expect pushback that regular change will cause a perceived issue but keep in mind that a delay that results in a larger change will cause greater issue and inefficiencies from misalignment.

Culture: Meticulous and Investigative

"Process Strategy":

Start with a single value stream to prove how vast the impact can be. Do not give up easily and spend time socializing the benefits as the capability builds. Make certain to document the change and the value that is brought from the change, both through the analysis and again once the value is achieved. Use this capability and foundation to prepare for the organizational change, once accepted the change can often go viral and overload the core team, so be prepared.

PLANT PLANNING

Inventory is a net result of actions. Planning production at the plant drives the vast majority of inventory efficiencies or inefficiencies. Here it is not only about Operational Excellence, it is about effective tradeoffs. By planning effectively, the production flow will be efficient. Downtime will be nearly eliminated, changeovers will be decreased, and most of all - overall inventory turns will be at all-time highs.

"Quick win" projects:

1. Plant planning is an area where successful change requires a "go and see" mindset and the ability to work directly with the planners. Look to encourage and build relationships but do not provide advice or look to make changes yet. These relationships are pivotal in the change management so do not overlook this step. If not able to spend time face to face at the plant, assign a leader to do this and empower them with the ability to drive the project. It is important for the lead of the project to show enough care to take the time and learn the process from those that are doing it and not via a teleconference. While on site be sure to walk the production lines being scheduled in such a manner that there is a clear understanding to what are physical barriers versus what are mental or status quo limitations.

    Theoretical return: This is a prerequisite to successful change implementations. While no direct return from the process it's imminent to any future ROI.

2. Review and recap what has now been learned with broader supply chain leadership. If all are in agreement, some of this information can also be shared strategically with some of the broader GMS leaders. In addition, look to identify talent to lead the project where needed. Develop these talented individuals by sharing the concepts and strategies with them, this will help get them aligned with the goals and encourage them to take pride and ownership and to become bold in their decisions. Let them be a part of the solution that will drive the change. At this point the company could also look to bring in subject matter experts

to consult on the project and fill any talent gaps found within the company.

> *Theoretical return: Again, little financial ROI up to this point but this is such an impactful change alignment is necessary to attain proper resourcing and support to make a sustainable change. It can also be expected that providing the visibility to the status quo will drive leaders and team to want to drive change, especially when they see they are not alone.*

3. Finally action can be taken. Start to plan and understand root cause of ineffective planning. In all cases and all levels of maturity there are always abilities to improve. Also keep in mind that the production environment is ever changing and that planning should be agile enough to respond appropriately.

Lay out the current planning process using the value stream mentality. Make it physically visible to the core team (put it on paper up on a wall, etc.) so that everyone can follow the flow and question why certain steps happen and why other steps are not incorporated. This will help understand what steps of planning are cohesive and which have gaps or need the greatest support. Look to create sub-teams to review and recommend improvements.

> *Theoretical return: The work done here will define the return of the overall effort, don't short the diligence.*

4. Once a clear layout of the value stream is complete and sub teams are ready to start the core team may need to prioritize work. Look to prioritize based on workloads. First reduce workload of the planners so that they can see benefit to what is happening. Confirm that the targeted

projects look to address the areas of lowest maturity and look to bring these in line with the broader process.

Strategically balance this with the path that the overall process needs to take and ensure that the sub teams align their processes to be able to deliver the overall paradigm shift. External support is most valued in this area by bringing in subject matter experts that have a non-biased view over the whole end to end process and they can help guide and mentor all the sub teams to ensure cohesiveness.

Theoretical return: Likely one of the higher overall ROIs companywide. Do not forget to measure and assign resources appropriately. Measure areas such as inventory savings, changeover savings/production efficiencies, and cost down/cost avoidance in logistics, along with any other opportunities identified by the team.

"Quick Win" Predecessors: A developed root cause process will help drive the right subprojects within the proper levels of maturity.

"Game Changer" project:

By increasing the maturity of production planning it opens doors for the opportunity to start exploring optimization and patterning strategies. In addition it can lend well to agility and cash to cash aspirations. The true game changing processes come from optimization of the manufacturing process in unconventional ways. For example: aligning multiple back shop and supplier processes so that inventory arrives reliably and just in time to key areas. This can also help identify ways to initiate a simple pattern production strategy in supporting areas that can results in better optimized supply, capacity, changeover, *and end-to-end inventory.*

"Game Changer" predecessors: High levels of maturity, agility, and effectivity in production planning processes.

Continuous Improvement Environment:

Strong production processes are ever-changing, looking to incorporate the newest capabilities or products and adjusting to customer needs. Production planning should do the same. It should always be on the forefront of the best processes and be looking for opportunities to improve.

Culture: Change Management and Diligence

"Process Strategy":

Improved efficiencies of planning will be contagious. The benefits will quickly spread across the company and become practically immeasurable. Inventory savings, changeover/manufacturing savings, and logistics efficiencies can all be measured and attributable to improved planning techniques. Measure these and make these visible, especially to leadership, so that there is a clear awareness to the importance of effective planning. It is not uncommon to hear everyone agree to this but action to continuously review and improve is often forgotten. This will arguably be one of the higher overall ROIs companywide out of all the proposed paradigm shifts so be sure to keep it top of mind for everyone.

PREBUILD PLANNING TO COVER RISK ON DOWNTIME

Prebuild planning is usually done by a plant based on their direct needs with little to no visibility or understanding from external or peripheral risks. Prebuilds almost always contain some type of extra inventory production as a buffer, yet not uncommon that the target is insufficient. As a result, the next prebuild buffer is more aggressive until excessive waste or budget issues result in arbitrary cuts or constraints that start a repeat of the same behaviors that got them in trouble to begin with. An end-to-end oversight and scenario planning can have a dramatic improvement in the overall process and inventory. This overarching global inventory planning capability is able to have a better understanding of the overall impact. It will also provide a better understanding impacting other levels within the supply chain, and visibility to the risk and variability that may not normally be visible or understood. Taking steps towards reducing end-to-end prebuild risks and expenditures can result in overall manufacturing and supply efficiencies that can mature into new opportunities in agility and productivity.

"Quick win" projects:

1. While not necessary to "go see," a clear understanding of what the planners are doing and what information they have at their disposal will be important to understand the status quo and identifying the proper root causes where ineffective outcomes prevail. This will also help the core leaders and teams to prioritize for the greatest returns.

    Theoretical return: This is a prerequisite to successful change implementations. While no direct return from the process it's imminent to any future ROI.

2. Take this step as a pre-work step to set up the proper path and change management. Projects will take less work and project time to shift processes but the bulk of time invested

will lie in change management and validation of the new concepts by experts to ensure unintended consequences or repercussions of change are lower than the current process. Balance prioritization of projects between the very quick wins and more mature and complex processes. Try to tackle the low hanging fruits of the quick wins to help build the momentum.

Theoretical return: This is a prerequisite to successful change implementations. While no direct return from the process it is imminent to any future ROI.

3. Provide more visibility and better information to planners so that they can make more educated decisions on prebuilds. Allocate resources and time to mentor planners on how this new information will be beneficial for them and show them how it will improve results. Look for feedback and provide flexibility in expectations so that they can absorb the concepts and align with the change. This will take limited work, resources, and very little change management.

Theoretical return: While actual return will be incremental it may also provide a pleasant and healthy return on time and investment.

4. Continuously increase expectations of improvements and measure the progress. Expand responsibilities and access for each planner watching to see what they do with the data and how they handle the responsibility. It will become obvious as to which planners were underutilized and which were already stretching to keep up. Look to leverage and challenge the underutilized to become first inceptors, leaders, and mentors. Work to free up more of their time

to focus on these improvements and pair them with centralized experts that can help build greater returns.

Theoretical return: Growth in return should be expected versus the prior step. Improving returns will be indicative of a good process, if return starts to dwindle review the current support and roadmap. The project direction or maturity was either too conservative or aggressive and the pace needs adjustment.

5. Opportunity is not done yet, once localized projects are kicked off and their foundations are stable it is time to look at a broader spectrum. Take similar steps to find the quick wins across the network. 1) Look to share findings of best practices and cross train additional planners on these best practices. 2) Integrate global planning information to further improve decisions that may have heavy impact up or downstream of the prebuild decision. 3) Review timing of these decisions and develop policies and training that enables the deferment of these decisions as long as possible, making the decisions as close to the production as possible. This may mean that more decisions made remain flexible and are firmed up at the last minute. 4) Review opportunities to improve planning tools linked to prebuilds. Look to enhance current software or to supplement with tools that can help triangulate information and improve decisions.

Theoretical return: This will likely see the greatest return due to scope but requires the foundation for maturity to be laid at the localized planning for to be effectively administered.

"Quick Win" Predecessors: Foundations in plant planning are a must otherwise all work done on prebuilding will be

heavily deteriorated or fall apart without a maturity in plant planning that is equal or higher than the target prebuild improvement strategy.

"Game Changer" project:

Production optimization and patterning programs exist that provide a genuine competitive advantage and that truly do work if set up properly. Software companies and corporations alike, struggle to sell and implement the best programs due to the complexity. *Specific levels of process and data maturity are required for such programs to stabilize. Most companies have not yet met this level of maturity and this is why it can be such a competitive advantage.*

"Game Changer" predecessors: High levels of maturity within supply planning process along with key talent that exhibit high levels of subject matter expertise and strategic problem solving skills.

Continuous Improvement Environment:

Look to establish a highly inquisitive and interactive environment that has a passion for sharing. Develop this through demonstrating how these attributes improve the quality of their work and odds of success. Acknowledge and reward efforts and behaviors that achieve targeted improvements and results.

Culture: Excellence and Collaborative

"Process Strategy":

Improved efficiencies will have a considerable improvement in inventory positions (prebuilt cycle stock and safety stock), reduced expedite fees, and ultimately free up cash flow and space. Comparatively a low investment for the rewards reaped. Approach this strategy with passion and exemplify the benefits wherever possible. Look to use these stretch projects to find underutilized talent and develop the leadership pipeline. Those that demonstrate intelligence and leadership traits here may be eligible to help lead larger and more complex strategies to come.

OBSOLESCENCE

Letting inventory go obsolete is the epitome of waste. Not only is there cost with the loss of the product itself, resulting waste has also consumed production capacity and other resources that have now been wasted. Sunken logistics cost and consumed raw material resources could have also been allocated to better use. Additional costs come with the disposal of the obsolete inventory. Eliminating obsolescence as a priority will improve both top and bottom line profits and adds benefits in many of the peripheral operations.

"Quick win" projects:

1. Improve obsolescence management by making risks visible through impact of batch sizes, and safety stock strategies. Develop accurate obsolescence risks projections by SKU. The ability to measure changes to the outcome of

obsolescence is a must. Advance the ability to see root cause of write off and obsolescence by SKU and focus improvements by addressing largest dollar impacts first.

Theoretical return: Greatest benefit and return will be for logistics due to the impact to the bottom line. As for cash flow impact the inventory gains can be immense but ensure the proper budgeting and do not overlook the costs that operations will need to carry.

2. Change policies to be more prescriptive and not global or generic. Use of attribute based rules in setting safety stocks. For example, using safety time instead of days on hand safety stock targets will improve efficiencies in some environments. Enabling more prescriptive policies will reduce write-off risk without major change or expense. Some of the easiest policies to address will be future policies such as batch size planning and minimum order quantities of new products to improve utilization in growth and mature phases of the product.

Theoretical return: Strong bottom line impact for logistics with an even stronger impact to cash flow and inventory. If done properly, operating costs should neutralize and provide a slight increase to operations agility.

3. Know and understand unintended consequences of KPI's. Production targets, ship to promise attainment, and absorption strategies, etc. will all impact downstream inventory and logistics costs. Provide broader insight to a balanced measurements and a report that shows the most optimized balance between upstream savings and downstream costs, and vice versa.

Theoretical return: An optimized result will likely have overall the most savings but may come with increased costs in some areas to save in others. Be prepared to influence budgets adjustments and to modify goals appropriately.

"Quick Win" Predecessors: Avoid perceptions that obsolescence reduction programs are contingent on other processes. This strategy should be standalone and only contingent on the value returned for the effort.

"Game Changer" project:

Implement a culture or passion to abolish obsolescence without negative impact to the standard business. Any negative impact is fully offset by a positive gain enabled by the change. For example if line absorption is negatively impacted, re-optimize the plan so that the mid-long term impact is a net gain. Implement robust countermeasures and empower teams to act using countermeasures to avoid obsolescence expense.

"Game Changer" predecessors: mature production planning with scenario optimization capabilities, continuous improvement policy of obsolescence, and low hanging fruits of quick win projects attained.

Continuous Improvement Environment:

Implement a continuous process to proactively identify gaps that could lead to obsolescence. Look to remove risks before waste is created. Try to make as many changes upstream of the original production as possible to attain the greatest benefit before any loss of resources have been realized.

Culture: Kiazen - Six Sigma

"Process Strategy":

Obsolescence is a source of pure waste. Look to improve production and process planning to avoid any obsolescence risks and loss of value. This will improve any businesses bottom line no matter how significant or insignificant the obsolescence may seem at face value. There is no excuse where pure waste should be allowed to exist by design.

POOLING

Strategies around the pooling of variability up stream impact more than just safety stocks. It can provide efficiencies across GMS that drive continuous cost down strategy opportunities and agility opportunities. There are many give-take analysis decisions to be made within a pooling strategy such as square footage of plant costs/labor costs/absorption costs through line utilization/logistics costs/inventory holding costs/warehousing costs across all locations and other smaller costs such as planning/oversite/peripherals etc. For now let us take simpler steps within the course correction and cover more mature policies such as deferment, delayed differentiation, and postponement in later chapters (yes these are similar but all three are different concepts). Some of the following concepts may seem to have attributes of these policies but keep in mind that pooling concepts set the foundation to be able to implement these policies as maturities build.

"Quick win" projects:

1. A cognitive planning process without a formal change or use of deferment systems can be a simple step to attain some pooling of inventories. When inventories are pooled together they create flexibility. Work with planners and encourage them to take actions to adjust where they are pooling inventory by developing operating procedures, work instructions, and training that encourages a pooling of inventory upstream of multiple locations in an attempt to pool inventory.

    Measure and watch this process in order to manage an unintended consequence such as increased expedites. If unintended consequences start to outweigh the benefits for a particular area look to work with the planners to make tweaks. Do not scrap the program, but rather address the single issue, as this training and concept will help build the confidence and skillsets necessary to start a deferment implementation.

    Theoretical return: A foundational step that can see varied return. Many supply chains overlook this process and gain immense value while others may have a more regular and rigorous review and see less gain but see the value in faster growth in system maturity.

2. Compare and review policies of safety stock stores and their physical locations. This step should not be real sophisticated and does not need to leverage the use of planning or optimization algorithms but it will take time and diligence. This should be a common sense review to where and why inventory stores are in place. Look to understand

and challenge while asking why and why not. While this is a simple request look to leverage the most critical thinkers that can synthesize the process and the concept and allocate the time for them to do so. This will start to develop the understanding to why and where inventory buffers exist.

Overall this may seem simple but it will set the stage for more fundamental programs like Single Echelon Inventory Planning (SEIP) and then Multi Echelon Inventory Planning (MEIO). It will also improve product flow and efficiencies as efforts look to place inventory buffers that may have been missed before. It is also likely to identify and reduce inventory buffers that are so large they become paralyzing for the location or at very least are tying up capital with limited return. Every company seems to find pockets of "forgotten" inventory that result in quick savings and ROI.

Theoretical return: Return comes in the rebalancing and flow of the inventory and in cost avoidance realized in manufacturing and logistics.

3. Consider working with suppliers as partners. Pooling of inventory at a supplier could be a great way of pooling the downstream variability or delaying the decision but it must be done in accordance with the attributes of the business.

Risks exist such as loss of visibility of inventory, added inefficiencies if the supplier is not motivated to properly manage the inventory, or if the supplier does not have the maturity or capacity to do so.

The benefits can be great where the pooling upstream, in this case the supplier being the only option, results in strong efficiencies. It also develops the fundamentals and opens opportunities to consider supplier owned and manage inventory or vendor managed inventory concepts. This pooling could be a result of the companies many internal consumption points that have offsetting variability. It could also be where the supplier sells the same item to many customers and by pooling the inventory at their location they can balance the demand much more effectively, and thus provide higher customer service to all.

Some of these concepts may make internal partners such as manufacturing, quality, or finance a little uneasy. Identify the first inceptors of the concept within a department that shows unease and work with those members to become change agents for the concept and look to acknowledge and address barriers that cause unease.

NOTE that this is NOT the same as Supplier Owned and Managed Inventory (SOMI). This concept works only in certain circumstances and can come with some very impactful negative consequences if the right attributes do not exist. If the right attributes exist it could be an immense opportunity but rarely works as a general policy.

Theoretical return: return will likely be shared between the company and the suppliers, pending on how it is set up. Saving provided for suppliers can be quantified and used in future negotiations.

"Quick Win" Predecessors: Likely not the highest benefit compared to other processes that can attain quick and easy return but these foundations become predecessors for more mature concepts.

"Game Changer" project:

Organize these policies and processes to start the skeleton of pilot program similar to its successor(s) to test the waters. If this shows potential it alludes to the company being ready for a more mature program and the exploration and proof of value can be kicked off. If unsuccessful don't give up, rather use this to root cause gaps in the supply chain and look to develop the maturity in that area.

> *"Game Changer" predecessors: A stable program and results that confirm the company is ready to increase its maturity in the area.*

Continuous Improvement Environment:

Opportunities for pooling can come from anywhere in the supply chain and should not be limited by scope or time or concept. Encourage team members to look outside the box and not be afraid to try and fail (ideally first validating the concept on paper).

Culture: Critical Thinking and Synthesis

"Process Strategy":

Use these strategies to stretch those with potential without major risk. Many of the concepts can be pitched on paper, reviewed, validated, and approved before physical action is taken. Talent development is key within supply chain so do not underestimate processes that can provide this strategy.

Implementing a few of these early concepts will help leaders and teams understand some of the barriers related to

the company maturity. By evaluating these concepts, and other similar ones, and implementing a few quick wins the core leaders can help address and rebalance the supply chain maturities. Do not get too aggressive and err on the side of projects that have less maturity. Trying to implement a quick win above the current maturity level will slow or limit the success and impede the value. Showing success in the initial steps is critical to setting the right strategy and to the overall success of the transformational journey.

CHAPTER 6

USE OF INVENTORY AS A STRATEGY

Inventory is a net result of action. The real meaning of this statement is that in order for inventory to exist there needs to be a decision, action, and then a result (inventory). Inventory is not a result that a company can instantaneously wish more or less of. It takes planning and strategy and time to deliver. As these strategies miss the mark or the planning gets off course the result is misaligned inventory. This could mean downtime at a plant or worse yet customer service level failures. It could also result in the opposite creating waste in excess inventory. It is inevitable for companies to face both circumstances at some point.

What differentiates the ineffective from the great is how they leverage this within their supply chain. Those supply chains that ranks poorly accept this as a part of doing business do nothing. The mediocre try to respond and the good try to proactively sense and respond. While the great implement programs that use these imbalances as strategic advantages.

It is not common to use a result such as inventory imbalance to drive strategic change but it is not impossible. In fact it may be easier than most want to believe. The easiest of these changes is to find synergies with parallel departments that can benefit from this and take advantage of those imbalances that are most frequent or unlikely to be able to be removed.

Logistics/Inventory Tradeoffs

There is a natural balance between speed and frequency of shipment and pipeline inventory levels. The faster and more frequent a shipment, the lower the pipeline inventory and vice versa. There is an optimal tradeoff that can be clearly identified.

This balance no longer needs to be mutually exclusive where one department must lose for the other to gain. In many cases a more complex approach can be taken, even when completed in a simplified approach, one step at a time. This approach looks at all parameters of inventory from supply to customer and along with all logistical options and parameters. If done correctly it provides win-win results for both inventory and logistics, ultimately increasing the company's bottom line.

"Quick win" projects:

1. Compile a matrix of timeframes and look to see where an imbalance occurs between inventory stores and shipment cadence by node (item-location). Possible timeframes that

can and should be considered is the minimum order quantity (converted to a number of days on hand), lot size (converted to a number of days on hand), production/packing frequency of the finished good, the number of days' supply necessary to ensure a full shipment, and the time cadence of shipments. In addition look to understand the inventory downstream that is held and the capability to put that inventory to use without increasing risk or impact to the customer.

Identify nodes where imbalances exist and then rank based on imbalance. Look to root cause a subset of imbalances with the highest impact. Take a few subsets at 10% increments down the list for the top 50% to compare and contrast the results and learn how opportunities may differ. Socialize these imbalances in an attempt to understand the impact and document why they may exist.

> *Theoretical return: A foundational step that can see varied return. Many supply chains overlook this process and gain immense value while others may have a more regular and rigorous review and see less gain but see the value in faster growth in system maturity.*

2. Take the newly defined list and root cause findings and now look to compile reasons and proposed changes to rebalance the timeframes. For example, a product may be packaged monthly but shipped quarterly and there is no reason for that other than misaligned planning. Then look to either increase shipping cadence to reduce inventory and improve flow or look to consolidate production runs into a larger and more efficient run. Keep in mind to prioritize the bottom

line dollar impact but do not forget to factor in the other potential implications.

> *Theoretical return: These opportunities often exist due to changes that are made over time within one GMS silo that are not properly communicated across the rest as a result return can be high and not difficult to achieve.*

3. Another key project is to use this information to supplement the discussion of inventory - logistics tradeoffs. Companies or teams may be inclined to cut transportation costs by changing mode transit (most likely a slower option) resulting in an increase to pipeline inventory without an understanding of the implications and costs. In reverse they may look to decrease inventory and intentionally or unintentionally increase the frequency of shipments or expedites without confirmation of the associated costs.

> *Theoretical return: Educating and encouraging informed decisions can be an effective way to reduce the overall landed cost impact of customer facing inventory.*

> *"Quick Win" Predecessors: No project or process predecessors are necessary but a robust and accurate data set will be pivotal to a successful outcome.*

"Game Changer" project:

Combine and challenge some of the most critical thinkers to look for savings by shifting, not adding inventory, into and out of the logistics network.   Can they reduce a downstream inventory buffer that is strategically in place due to an upstream bottleneck or strategic risk and move some of it into the logistical pipeline to decrease transit costs? Can they increase the speed of transit or planning with limited costs to reduce pipeline stock and free up cash flow? Can they identify more strategic opportunities to change the product flow, location of storage, or strategies such as Leapfrogging (explained later) or others? Don't limit the opportunities based on the skill or maturity necessary. Rather use these potential opportunities to articulate the value of increasing skill and maturity.

> *"Game Changer" predecessors: A stable program and results that confirm the company is ready to increase its maturity in the area. Team may also need guidance and mentorship from either internal subject matter experts or consultants. Do not be afraid to validate findings through a review and validation by experts or consultants as this will help support the validity of the team's efforts when they are challenged by peers or other leaders.*

Continuous Improvement Environment:

Due to the ever-changing environment and network for both inventory and logistics this should be a standard process that has a regular refresh and cadence. It is not likely to be a daily activity but should be recognized as a value proposition and opportunity that teams look to own as a way to provide value and return.

Culture: Discerning and Motivated

"Process Strategy":

Use these strategies to free up cash flow and drive bottom line growth, impact will be high for effort put forth if done correctly. Also look to imbed these opportunities as foundational items that can support the alignment and change management necessary to drive a transformational paradigm shift in GMS.

PROCUREMENT/INVENTORY STRATEGY

Procurement traditionally has 2 levers when in negotiation with suppliers; time and cost. In order to get costs down, traditionally commitment or frozen PO time went up due to larger batches (commodity of scale -CoS) and negotiated service time (reducing risk on supplier for orders placed upstream). In order to get time down, costs would go up due to smaller batch size (reduced CoS) and increased risk of preorder or prebuild. Through visibility and collaboration with inventory planning, procurement can more effectively negotiate successful contracts with high success of service, picking suppliers with lowest variability and knowing where to push and when to pull between cost and time, thus impacting inventory owned by the company.

"Quick win" projects:

1. Articulating the value in this case starts by understanding the company's policies when it comes to procurement. By understanding the policies it will be easier to find common ground and articulate value through collaboration. Build a relationship with a few procurement reps that will be most open to developing collaborative efforts. It does not seem like a project in itself but it takes commitment especially if there currently is no perceived connection or collaboration. This is the first step in building maturity. If this is

overlooked it will make alignment in upcoming steps more difficult.

> *Theoretical return: A foundational step as it is easy to overlook the basic needs to build a relationship and show how collaboration can add value.*

2. Compile a matrix of policy comparisons and gaps along with possible opportunities to define change. Start to build a core team that can correct, add, and validate the matrix. Then look to rank and prioritize the efforts based on maturity. Start small and build the relationship and maturity through a "quick win" collaborative effort. Do not forget to socialize and educate on the opportunities. Continue to develop teams and progressively work through these projects. Once gains or opportunities start to slow, revisit the initial steps, reassess, and revamp the matrix. With the new and more educated collaboration the matrix will perpetually mature just as the development of both departments.

> *Theoretical return: A foundational step as it is easy to overlook the basic needs to build a relationship and show how collaboration can add value.*

3. Once the newly formed relationship with procurement is strengthened and some quick win projects have gained favor look to partner to identify additional opportunities. Weigh out give-take opportunities in addition to win-win opportunities and socialize these with leaders articulating the net gains. Do not present them individually, present together with all leaders in the room so the gains are prevalent and concern are addressed collaboratively.

Theoretical return: By building the open collaboration it will quickly grow the maturity developing further opportunities. Expect positive impacts on inventory levels, improvements in supply reliability, and less work for the procurement team along with some changing metrics.

4. If and when maturity improves and optimization programs exist in the inventory space look to integrate procurement decisions into these optimization scenarios before the decisions are made. This will help provide a broader understanding of the implications of these decisions and improve the overall supply chain.

   Theoretical return: Each of these decisions will provide perpetual return. Immediate ROI may not be prevalent but as more decisions are made in this manner sustainable returns will lower overall costs and improve the supply chain.

"Quick Win" Predecessors: No project or process predecessors are necessary but a good working relationship and good data will facilitate the success.

"Game Changer" project:

Integrate inventory and procurement decisions as early into the supply chain as possible. This means that partnering these two teams is pivotal. Once the relationship, understanding of the interdependent processes, and ability to understand and define accurate results are accomplished it is time to expand the opportunity.

Create a partnership between inventory and procurement teams together in order to collaborate with research and development (R&D) teams. Approach this as a service to R&D, enabling them to focus on the R&D while being assured simplified access to the best products that are sustainable for commercialization. By consulting network planning this new collaboration can effectively drive a full paradigm shift of the supply chain one new product at a time.

> *"Game Changer" predecessors: A stable program and relationship between inventory and procurement are pivotal. By working multiple quick win projects together they will develop a clear and educated understanding of the cause-effect relationship between their decisions. This will be necessary to ensure no misguided decisions result in failures for R&D.*

Continuous Improvement Environment:

Provide an environment that encourages cross pollination. Also look to reward such action and discourage any refusals to support these teams. Challenge these teams to develop and train other teams and relationships. The core team may take the approach of continuous growth and division.

Culture: Cross-Pollination and Service Oriented

"Process Strategy":

Put less effort and concern on highly mature products and service relationships. Rather look to focus and make the most gains on the newest products with the largest inventory spend. Ideally the strategy influences the original decisions as far back as the initial R&D stage to prevent rework or renegotiation later in the commercialized process.

INVENTORY/SALES BALANCE

"If I give you an apple"- If I give you an apple it may make you feel pretty good. If I give you ten apples you may feel even better. But now how about I ask for a dollar in return? How about ten dollars for ten apples? You may still feel it is a fair deal and accept the exchange. How about you accept the gift and after you eat the single apple I say "you owe me *five* dollars". How would you feel? Worse yet, you give away the ten apples and feel you are sharing the gift, but after such a good deed I say "you owe me *one hundred* dollars for the apples". It may ruin the relationship.

Dysfunction between sales and supply chain can often come from a parallel concept. When sales is only concerned with sales opportunities and that results in bias in forecast or demand for additional inventories to not restrict potential sales it creates frustration for supply chain. In reverse when supply chain cannot meet its commitments it introduces pain and frustration to the sales teams.

Let us discuss a single apple as a single unit of inventory. Just like inventory, it has to be given before it can be consumed. It also has to arrive when needed otherwise alternatives are chosen and the opportunity is missed. Just like the apple, inventory comes with expense and a shelf life. Asking for it too early, at the wrong point, or for too much results in excess expense and waste just like paying five dollars for a single apple or one hundred dollars for ten. Additional holding costs, logistics costs, and opportunity costs of tied up inventory and capital result in exponential costs before the product is sold.

"Quick win" projects:

1. Metrics, not KPIs, will be an important step to building this relationship. Both teams are very intelligent teams but speak very different languages. Look to build some quick and simple measurements of inventory availability and use. Leverage current inventory metrics and sales metrics to create a combined metric. Socialize the metric, without verbalizing its intent, to see what the response is. Capture the questions and bring them back to see if they influence or impact the underlying intent. Adjust the metric accordingly until the intent behind the metric will be easily seen and articulated. The metric should be intuitive, provide the proper support, and clearly show actionable benefit.

   Theoretical return: Visibility and understanding always provides value. Don't give up and don't sell the process short.

2. Utilize aforementioned metrics to start small. This is an area where a big bang implementation will nearly always fail. Build relationships with a few team members from each side and socialize the impact. Do not define an expected change, rather encourage the cross functional pairs to discuss and define how they can influence and change. Then have each pair pitch their ideas to the other pairs.

   Theoretical return: This guerilla warfare approach will drive maturity and understanding and slowly change the culture. This approach may take more work but will ensure success where a big bang approach is likely to cause more harm to the relationship and interactions than benefit.

3. Implement the best idea but start small with one sales team at a time looking for implications to develop before expanding to other teams. It may be possible to implement a couple ideas simultaneously in different teams. This could help define which ones are more successful and can be implemented more broadly. It also breaks the ice for these other teams. Many of the ideas will likely be collaborative visibility, so be prepared to support them with the proper processes and technologies. Invest appropriately and consider bringing in change management experts to mentor the implementing teams.

   Theoretical return: There is a heavy change management effort but in the greater aspect of inventory costs or sales opportunities the investment is trivial to the potential return.

4. Expose successful metrics to broader leadership teams moving them from the awareness stage to an actionable stage. As actions start to be taken, document how these actions impact the measurement positively. Showing that the metric is accurate and can be influenced proactively will increase in importance for the company and eventually will be a supporting performance indicator or a Key Performance Indicator (KPI) for the broader leadership.

   Theoretical return: Broader exposure will drive sustainability and prevent teams to reverting back to their old ways once focus is reduced and core teams move to the next project.

"Quick Win" Predecessors: No predecessors are necessary but relationships are important to sales and to the success of the projects. Do not underestimate the power of building

these relationships but don't allow the relationships to overshadow the analytics or the overall goal.

"Game Changer" project:

Integrate optimization and sales planning software cross functionally between sales and inventory. Do not confuse this step with Sales and Operations Planning (S&OP). Also, do not expect that team or others to drive this effort.

For example, while programs like demand sensing are often viewed as a sales forecasting tool they actually provide exponentially higher value in production and inventory planning. It is not always easy for sales to adjust forecasts outside of frozen windows using shorter term signals like demand sensing. Although it is beneficial for shorter term production and inventory planning as they can balance risk rewards and implement plans with countermeasures if the risks are realized.

In return inventory and planning programs and metrics, especially those that have proactive elements, can provide much needed insights to sales and forecasting. Sales can utilize these data feeds to implement different strategies. Strategies could include promotions to chase upside where excess inventory is available (demand shaping), avoid promoting costs where inventory cannot support enough sales lift to offset the promotion expense, or switch sales and marketing efforts and forecasts quicker by triangulating their metrics with those from GMS. Again, for some companies this may seem like S&OP efforts but these should not be single efforts by a single team rather be broader collaborative efforts utilizing the expertise across the business.

"Game Changer" predecessors: A stable program and relationship between inventory and sales will ensure success. Use the guerilla warfare approach and be cautious not to push it along too quickly before the maturity of some quick wins have been established and successful.

Continuous Improvement Environment:

Provide an environment that encourages and enforces efficient and effective actions. Utilize metrics and supporting performance measurements to drive changes in KPIs and ensure accountabilities are aligned. Keep accountability strong by rewarding efforts through broad visibility to the gains created through action taken and to which employees these successes can be attributable.

Culture: Modeling Leadership and Visible Reward

"Process Strategy":

Use the guerilla warfare approach and be cautious not to push it along too quickly before the maturity of some quick wins have been established and successful. Use visible rewards to mature the strategies.

These visible rewards may not need to be monetary rather a visible recognition of effort. Monetary rewards should come through incremental sales and reduced inventories driving increased compensations to those whom the gains are attributed. If this is not the case for the business then the benefits derived from their efforts should be acknowledged appropriately through monetary benefits where possible. This collaboration is too important to neglect the efforts invested.

THE S&OP ADVANTAGE THROUGH DEMAND SHAPING

Demand shaping is a countermeasure that can be put into place (often through S&OP or SIOP outputs) to take advantages of prior missteps or calculations that result in inventory issues. The most common steps in demand shaping are use and timing of promotions (advertising, promotions, discounts, or sales incentives) to offset an overage or shortage of inventory. The common practices within demand shaping have to be used cautiously and strategically as it often just "moves" the imbalance to a time it can be more easily absorbed and does not remove the issue.

"Quick win" projects:

1. Gather knowledge and reasoning as to why and how current promotions are implemented. This will help define where to start and what to influence. In addition look to understand historical inventory trends to see where the gravest imbalances exist. It is likely more successful to start in an area of the business that is most likely to address inventory when creating a promotion strategy in conjunction with an area that have the have heavy inventory flux and has the most difficulty controlling excess inventory when it develops.

   Theoretical return: This again is a heavy change management lift so due diligence will go a long ways towards the success and will the investment even if the return is not perceived to exist.

2. Once some due diligence is completed, compile a cross functional team from the areas of highest likelihood to collaborate. Gather a cross functional team together face to face and hold an "improvement" event with the group to identify the perceived issues. Acknowledge up front that the majority of the issues that will be found cannot be solved by this group. Through this process it will help drive understanding and alignment that not all root causes are easy to solve or that they can wait for others to solve their resulting problems. The intent is to foster a collaborative coalition that looks to face what now becomes clear as their problems.

    Theoretical return: Through this process it will help drive understanding and the need to countermeasure and balance risks out of this teams control and motivate the team to collaborate in a responsive mode.

3. Identify the most educated and passionate members from the event to develop a core subgroup and make remaining members a part of the extended team. Leverage their passion and challenge them to change their own destiny. Challenge them to put together a communication plan that addresses the inventory imbalance problem. Remind them this communication plan has to be to drive action in the future that will reduce or remove the current inventory issue. Drive them to develop a sustainable process that addresses future inventory imbalances through the same process. As a result one of the likely and few options they

have to meet this criterion are to develop a demand shaping concept.

> *Theoretical return: There is a heavy change management effort but in the greater aspect of inventory costs or sales opportunities the investment is trivial to the potential return.*

4. Address the WIIFM of sales by showing the value of demand shaping. Show how now the budgets are balanced, cash flows are quicker and cleaner, and capacity remains more aligned. Advocate allocating savings supported by sales to improve supply agility and ensure the right product, at the right place, and at the right time. Projects that enable a closer just in time (JIT) approach to production or product differentiation will enable sales to chase more upside and not spend as much time trying to recover misses in other products. While demand shaping has some aspects of "sell what you got" it is a proactive approach that enables a "sell what the customer wants and we can deliver" mentality.

> *Theoretical return: This is still considered a quick win due to the fact it only advocates for change, taking less effort and providing less return than delivering an actual process changing project.*

"Quick Win" Predecessors: Demand shaping is fairly unique from other projects but it does take a heavy level of relationship building and change management skills. Even though no specific projects are required as predecessors, consider implementing a few projects and building relationships before taking on a demand shaping strategy.

"Game Changer" project:

Drive savings and opportunity though demand shaping but focus on the long term goal of how demand shaping can create a paradigm shift in supply with the support of sales. This is a huge win for sales as momentum builds. The cost of these demand shaping promotions, along with the supply chain savings needs to be clear and visible. These savings need to advocate for bigger change.

The game changer project is actually beyond the demand shaping process itself, it is the implementation of projects to reduce the need for demand shaping that creates a leaner, agile, and more effective manufacturing and supply environment. In addition, proficient demand shaping programs in semi-mature to mature states can help enable further production effectiveness through production patterning, production optimization, and production wheel concepts.

> *"Game Changer" predecessors: Demand shaping development and maturity are key predecessors so ensure a proper and stable foundation. Drive a commitment to demand shaping before initiating discussion on more mature production strategies.*

Continuous Improvement Environment:

Visibility to the value demand shaping brings will be important to the sustainability of the concept. Ensure metrics are in place and understood. Perpetually maintain and report out the demand shaping actions and results. This will help educate and inform the veteran members while initiating the new members.

It shows one of the costs of inefficiency or poor decisions. In addition it will provide valuable insight and support necessary to drive game changing projects throughout the company.

Culture: Aggressive Action and Awareness

"Process Strategy":

Demand shaping development and maturity are necessary to drive some of the mature strategic projects. Take a second look and dig deeper into the future aspirations before discounting the value of a demand shaping concept or strategy. If the right foundation is set for demand shaping it can be a cornerstone to support future projects and sustain future risks, especially those that could result in over production of a segment of inventory.

BALANCE BETWEEN INVENTORY AND FINANCIALS

Inventory planning and management is the largest impact to cash flows in many cases. Inventory not only impacts cash flow but also stock price, project ROI's, Return on Cash (ROC), Return on Assets (ROA), margin, budgets, and future target - not to mention inventory positions are indicative of the health of the company (especially for Wall Street). The team needs to be able to accurately identify future inventory positions and related costs. If they cannot, the future budget or income projections would likely be noticeably incorrect compared to actual results. By not being able to dial in accurate inventory projections it puts stress on financial reporting, either resulting in considerable conservatism in financial planning or creating a noticeable impact to the financial accuracy. Whether the financial miss was positive or negative a noticeable impact can negatively impact the stock price. A financial miss, positive or negative, is identified as company instability and is correlated with investment risk. It also creates many questions by investors, including the ability of the leadership and the control they have over the company. The confidence in leadership and financial stability can represent nearly half of the P/E ratio risk an investor is willing to take on and thus it is important to be able to forecast accurate inventory levels and financial impacts.

"Quick win" projects:

1. Financials are heavily dependent on inventory so advocate for a partnership with the finance team as support and avocation for all process and strategy changes. This becomes the first quick win project as people will always be a big part of being able to implement changes in process and technology. Finance is not a rule enforcer rather a partner to help the company exceed its profit targets.

   Theoretical return: This step should be easy and change management efforts should be fairly low. Check emotions at the door as finance may have some hard truths to share but this is where the value really comes in.

2. Finance unfortunately gets the harder job to drive costs down and profit up but has a mixed ability to drive them through power. As a result strong finance team members will have a heavy degree of change management ability and depth in industry knowledge. Downside is they may not speak the same language as some of the other partners. Build liaison relationships with finance and use their

mentorship and big picture guidance to define some of the upcoming inventory and supply chain strategies.

Theoretical return: Surprisingly ROI will be quite high as the team often has a broader reach and understanding than most and a strong willingness to help as they need financial stewards throughout the company, especially those that understand cash flow and inventory.

3. Identify finance team members, especially those younger in their career, to help lead and drive some of the strategic inventory projects. Assign them inventory projects that do not necessarily have direct reduction on inventory but those that require strategic tradeoffs such as projects that involve a balanced give-take between inventory and logistics or procurement. This provides some neutral ground and factual approach with the bottom line impact at the core. It will also help with the alignment and buy in from finance when budgets need to be realigned.

    Theoretical return: Taking on inventory projects with a team finance tie will help bring importance, visibility, and a financial focus to the project, ultimately increasing probability of success and increasing their knowledge of inventory challenges.

4. Inventory reporting is a basic requirement for both finance and inventory therefore every company has some type of reporting. The key is developing the reporting that makes companies great. Great companies can proactively see inventory changes and the corresponding financial impacts well into the future. This makes companies great because of the maturity it entails. It is not easy and it relies heavily on the strength and maturity of many other sales and

supply chain reports. If the contributing reports are of poor quality, finance and inventory projections will suffer, ultimately impacting the value of the company.

Compile all of the financial and inventory reporting currently available. Review the current maturities and identify gaps. Put together a project charter to address the gaps and build to a level of maturity. Once complete revisit the assessment and look to see if there are new levels of reports that could be developed.

This will slowly but continuously improve the impact and value to the company. Articulate and publish the value of doing so, then look to attain support to incorporate this practice a standard of work for the company. Develop a process and accountability within both departments to integrate this into their standard work duties with the proper allocation and support to continuously improve it.

> *Theoretical return: Key projects and optimizations such as financial optimization, target inventory positions, SEIP, MEIO, and costing strategies are all dependent on the success of financial inventory reports. Thus the return is high as it enables further success in these (and other) areas.*

"Quick Win" Predecessors: No predecessors are necessary but financial changes cannot stand alone and need to be done in conjunction with the proper maturity. Be sure to incorporate other strategies that will help support and maintain the savings/value created through the projects developed with the finance team.

"Game Changer" project:

Financial optimization of inventory is a higher level maturity project but can have great payback and success when collaboratively driven by inventory and finance teams. In conjunction with this optimization, a new paradigm of inventory and financial reporting can come to reality putting the overall business in a new league. Leading companies will utilize forward looking inventory and financial reports to drive key business strategies and ultimately drive the value of the company.

> *"Game Changer" predecessors: Functionality of game changing inventory and financial projects all rely on current inventory and financial reporting capacities and peer collaboration. Ensure the highest possible maturities in these areas.*

Continuous Improvement Environment:

Financial and inventory performance should be important to all employees. Be bold in the environment, make it visible and make it important. Profitability is why any of these efforts are put forth so don't let its importance fade. Some companies provide a stock quote in a public place to encourage growth and success, why stop there? What else can be made visible that will create the right motivation?

Culture: Intellectual and Broad Perspective

Drive visibility and understanding, drive collaboration, and drive passion through education and understanding of the "why." Encourage those who show pride and educate those who seem to not care. No one works for free so help them realize their value. Provide the reporting insight so they can measure their success. Provide the mentorship they need to attain their success.

STRATEGIC PLANNING USING TARGET INVENTORY POSITIONS (TIPS)

Target Inventory Positions can be a "holy grail" to supply chain if managed properly and accurately. A time dependent (stochastic) TIP can foresee what is changing in the supply chain and what magnitude of impact it may have on production needs, warehousing, financials & cash flows, budgets, scenario planning, health of customer orders (order prioritization), and ultimately supply chain health.

"Quick win" projects:

1. Basic cycle stocks are usually one of the easiest components of a TIP. In its simplest form a basic cycle stock for an item-location (node) is the greater of half of the batch size or half of the forecasted volume covered by the campaign timeframe. There are many conditions and team members that will challenge this as being too simple. It may likely be too simple but all processes and cycle stock concepts will need this information so start here.

Identify how difficult it is to attain, and maintain, this data regularly. Address roadblocks or limit scope to make it manageable. Measure and report this data on a regular basis for a forward looking 12 month period as a beta test. Compare this test to actual inventories every month. Actual cycle stocks may be difficult to isolate from other inventories so it may require summing other projected inventory positions and comparing them together but keep in mind it will make root cause analysis more difficult to pin down.

Treat this like forecasting the cycle stock at every node and measuring the error of that forecast. Focus on the error and identify what caused that error. Further identify how to measure that root cause and incorporate that into the cycle stock forecast measurement.

A common and high impact root cause is often a prebuild of inventory due to a capacity constraint or a strategic decision. Supply planning should have this information and be able to provide this data with accuracy. Do not look for perfection on day one. Audit and challenge what is given to ensure the proper process is taken to get the right inventory that has been pre-built. Often this results in multiple sources or data pulls to attain an accurate prebuild picture bit the added effort will pay off.

> *Theoretical return: Knowing how to project, influence, and control cycle stock creates a powerful tool that can influence and drive maturity improvements in planning and throughout the company.*

2. Work closely with manufacturing and logistics on pipeline inventories but do not expect them to own or drive this

analysis. Pipeline inventory is inventory that is in motion between nodes in the supply chain. The most common and highest volume of this type of inventory likely will be in transit outside of the four walls of the company sites. This is not the only pipeline inventory. Pipeline inventory can also exist on manufacturing lines and in warehouses awaiting a bottleneck in the manufacturing process. Do not confuse or mix this inventory with buffer stores of inventory such as safety stocks, even if these buffers are in a first in first out rotational process.

Measuring pipeline inventory is tricky, especially if there are lower levels of maturity in logistics reporting or inventory visibility within manufacturing sites. Projecting future pipeline inventory often consists of a more complex roll-up of forecasted demand to upstream nodes using bill of material (BOM) quantities. It is a highly involved process but if master data is accurate it is a fairly simple process. Pipeline inventory is then defined by multiplying the time spent in the pipeline from node to node (path) times the equivalent stochastic demand. Again not an easy compilation of a highly involved process and data set but ultimately not a difficult or complex calculation.

Compare the forecasted pipeline stock at every node to the reported actuals for the same time period and measuring the error of that forecast. Focus on the errors and identify what caused that error. Further identify how to measure that root cause and incorporate that into the pipeline stock forecast measurement.

Theoretical return: Be clear on the investment and involvement as this will take a lot to pull together. Return is also high as it brings advantages and visibility to all of GMS with other key consumers of the data being Operational Excellence, Finance, and all inventory metric audiences. Being a major part of the TIP it also provides considerable return in a broader use.

3. Basic safety stock forecasts may be as simple as pulling them right out of the planning or optimization systems and grossing to units. Keep in mind many system have more than one safety stock lever often allowing for different factors such as unit targets, days on hand targets, or time buffers. If necessary, add in any strategic inventory buffers put in places that are not accounted for in the safety stock store levers.

Compare this basic measurement to the total actual inventory being reported minus the actual inventory that was allocated to cycle and pipeline stocks. Measure the error to forecast and look to root cause deltas keeping in mind that some of these may be not to a root cause of an inventory buffer but also due to a miss in cycle or pipeline stocks.

Forecast error or bias in itself is often a driver of cause. Calculations will often start to incorporate known biases or errors in recent months until it can be accounted for and corrected outside the frozen production window. Spend further focus on the errors and identify what caused that error. Identify how to measure that root cause and incorporate that into the proper stock forecast measurement.

Theoretical return: Visibility to future inventory buffer stores is key to driving improvements, value, and strategy. It will uncover all decisions being made that drive inventory positions. Time spent providing this visibility will pay exponential dividends.

4. Combining all elements into a TIP is where the real value comes together. If accurate, this will provide immense value for many teams and leaders and quickly attain a very broad acceptance. It is as simple as combining all the parts to cycle, pipeline, and buffer/safety stocks and providing visibility over time.

   The accuracy must be understood as it will impact the amount of risk tolerance or risk mitigation necessary when making a decision. Provide metrics and visibility to forecasted TIPS and actuals over many lags. Work with the metrics teams to scope out the ability to replicate dashboards created for demand forecasting results or to create similar concepts. Please note and articulate that this is not a real forecast rather a compilation of planning results so errors or inefficiencies can be traced back to processes in planning with correctable results a highly mature and effective supply chain should be able to dial these future TIPS with very little error.

   Theoretical return: This capability should be critical to highly effective supply chains.

"Quick Win" Predecessors: No predecessors are necessary but a foundational level of maturity in reporting and data will be important. Actions can still be taken at any level of maturity but the effort will be higher and a lower maturity will result in a lower level of attainable accuracy.

"Game Changer" project:

Incorporate TIPs into the foundations of more mature strategies like dynamic order priority and allocation systems or inputs to demand sensing programs. Also, if accuracy is robust enough consider internal replenishments within planning systems or manual planning efforts. Keep in mind this will not replace real planning systems rather support them for items that cannot be planned traditionally or that are already on replenishment targets. This is the peak of the extended traditional inventory saw-tooth at point of replenishment and thus can be used in many aspects of the business.

> *"Game Changer" predecessors: Each element of inventory must be compiled and understood before an accurate TIP can be developed. Ensure proper maturity within each element as the whole will only be as strong as its weakest element.*

Continuous Improvement Environment:

Developing a TIP is a journey. It is common for businesses to attempt to throw one together in excel over a week's time but ultimately to find limited use as a directional element. An accurate TIP that can be used broadly is not complex but is very technical and takes a heavy focus to identify all moving parts and incorporate them appropriately.

Culture: Focus and Technical

"Process Strategy":

Commit to the long haul, value will come as soon as the process is started but do not slow down once momentum is started. This is a new concept and strategy to most so it will be easy to drop it and fall back into the status quo so keep focus and push for a continuous grind.

CHAPTER 7

THE INVENTORY PARADIGM SHIFT
USING INVENTORY AS A STRATEGIC ADVANTAGE

Inventory as a strategic advantage is a concept where the use of inventory can be used differently than before or than by the competitor. It requires an "intelligent" use of technology and resources. In addition it must be robust, usable, and sustainable. Lastly, it must be unique and difficult to repeat without the right recipe and cultivation.

In the case of inventory, intelligence means many things. It means that a process or technology can proactively address future needs, and integrate more information. It also means that management and process exceeds the average or standard. In general it means possessing the capability to understand or deal with new or challenging situations. Ultimately intelligence is relevant to another subject, process, or item therefore one must look to improve the intelligence relevant to the current status quo.

Usability of processes and technology to drive inventory intelligence must be robust and comprehensive enough to manage the nuances of the supply chain, yet have outcomes that are consumable by the teams managing them. The best algorithms in the world are useless unless someone uses the results. This often means stripping down the intelligence of the algorithm to meet comprehension of the current talent pool. Whether this, or the opposite, is true – it is healthier and easier to increase the maturity of one than to decrease the maturity of the other.

Building intelligence, maturity, usability, and strategic advantages are all relative to past measurements. They all take time and a concerted effort to integrate a change. This is why the concept of continuous improvement works well in many areas. Look to build these capabilities through continuous improvements using a clear strategy to attain complex changes or large paradigm shifts.

For example, the "internet of things" can have a new meaning when applied toward inventory. Often viewed as complex and risky, the concept of integrating all machines into a highly interactive and responsive network can be overwhelming and even scary to think about. Yet, this capability enables broad visibility and understanding of all inventory stores, buffer, bottlenecks, wastes, and shortages. This can all be done at the tip of a fingertip without the need to wait for someone to respond or compile a library of analytics to attain the answer to a simple request. Use it, and use it wisely by fitting technology and an intertwined inventory internet of things into each progressing project and reporting capability to break down the complexity and build the maturity.

Using inventory to develop a paradigm shift towards collaborative and strategic advantages takes a concerted effort by all team members to collaborate intelligently, think strategically, and embrace complexity in a methodical and progressive approach. Implementing in this way should slowly stretch teams to new areas that once were well outside their comfort zones. It should not have limitations or barriers and should consider all opportunities. Not all opportunities fit in all situations so it will be important to completely understand the opportunity along with its strengths and weaknesses. There is not a one size fits all approach. Each situation, as its own, is looking to find the best strategy for the situation. In order to do so let's review a few possible strategies, their attributes, and ways to scope the process and fit for a given situation through some quick win opportunities. The greatest leaders must take educated risks to gain value so do not be afraid to try and fail but do not accept failure too easily.

SUPPLIER OWNED AND MANAGED INVENTORY (SOMI)

The concept of SOMI has been around a while and was developed for very good reason. Just because it is supplier owned and managed does not mean it must be at the supplier's site. Some of the greatest benefits of SOMI are that it not only puts the responsibility planning and service on the supplier but it also frees up cash flow by putting the inventory cost on the supplier's books. The downside is that the supplier now incurs many more expenses and will ultimately pass these costs on to the business through increases in cost of goods, premiums on costs that used to be pass through, like logistics costs, or by lowering the quality or service provided, either intentionally or unintentionally, as they look to cut cost to make up for the additional expense.

This concept can also be used as a service where a supplier with expertise and proper resources can warehouse and manage that inventory onsite as a service to the consuming company. Often this is akin to pay on consumption and it is common in hospitals or for repair parts in manufacturing where the inventory comes at a high cost or risk of obsolescence to the consuming company but a much lower cost or risk to the supplier.

"Quick win" projects:

1. Compile a list of as many suppliers as possible. Organize and rank them on three criteria, size of supplier's total business, annual sales to company, and trustworthiness. This should not be an exact science but do not ignore accuracy. Some procurement teams have robust versions of this already, if so then look to refresh and supplement where needed.

   Grading the supplier's total size of business relative to the other suppliers by use of scale of high, medium, low, or 1-10 will be sufficient. The annual spend the company makes on the supplier should be available from procurement or finance. Leave the measurement in financial terms and in this case it should be fairly accurate but does not have to be exact. A supplemental measurement that shows the percentage of spend vs. the total supply spend will also be handy. Last is trustworthiness. It will be likely there will be a need to start with instinctive scoring try to make it more scientific and less emotive. Look to planners and procurement to integrate supplier assessments, risk of origin, government impacts, and physical location into the analysis.

Theoretical return: A pivotal item that if clear and available will be used widely in supply chain decisions and strategies. Information will show benefit in the hands of logistics, procurement, planning, Operational Excellence, and of course inventory teams.

2. Use the compilation of supplier information to start a "what if" conversation with key partners. Invite innovative first inceptors from logistics, planning, procurement, and supply chain. This is a scoping conversation and no action should take place until the exercise is complete. As a team, develop a supplier ranking that will drive the likelihood of the supplier becoming a strong SOMI partner. There is no correct answer, if the ranking does not work then go back and try a different ranking. The intent of the ranking is to boil likely SOMI candidates to the top of the list for discussion.

A likely SOMI candidate should be of large size, higher reliability, and enough of a financial impact to attain ROI on the effort. Ideally a candidate supplier should have a better financial capability than the downstream entity as there needs to be mutually beneficial gain by the supplier carrying a higher financial burden and risk. Compile a list of the top candidates for SOMI conversations and start to socialize with a broader leadership but be sure to socialize the risks along with the benefits.

> *Theoretical return: Building the concept of working outside the company's walls will provide great gains in maturity. The value is not only in building a SOMI list but building a rigor and understanding of suppliers, many other ideas or actions may blossom for the momentum created here.*

3. Take the newly created list SOMI candidates and look to organize them by the benefit to the supplier. Look for the supplier that would benefit the most and work with the appropriate teams to see if they feel they can leverage this as a negotiation or what costs may come with it. Validate this information and then compare it to the expected gains. If there is a net benefit look to put together a project to make it happen on a small number of suppliers as a pilot. Look to watch the relationship until the benefits and any unintended consequences are clearly revealed.

> *Theoretical return: This pre-work and pilot will ensure the proper actions for the highest return when scaling the concept of SOMI. Expect lessons to be learned so for greatest benefit and return provide ample time to initiate the pilot and study its lessons.*

4. Review list of potential SOMI partners again. Now going a little deeper in the list compare strategies of Vendor Managed Inventory (VMI) as an alternative where consequences may outweigh return for SOMI, yet the expertise of the supplier could add value to the current planning and management of the inventory.

> *Theoretical return: While often overlooked, VMI returns can often exceed those of SOMI.*

"Quick Win" Predecessors: Concepts of pooling and initial pre-work for SOMI and VMI should be completed before a pilot for either is run. Strong education plans will also be important for success.

"Game Changer" project:

Look to expand and leverage SOMI only where the right fit exists. Expand the pilot concept to all suppliers where it provides the right value. An over expansion or premature set up has proven to be very costly. A well balanced management of suppliers through the use of standard supply relationships, pooling, SOMI, and VMI will result a highly effective model.

"Game Changer" predecessors: A stable pilot program that can clearly articulate the gains while identify and address unintended consequences.

Continuous Improvement Environment:

Look to review SOMI relationships every few years or at contract renewals. If set up correctly the supplier review and ranking becomes a highly impactful document that is supported and maintained across the company.

Culture: Subjective and Unbiased

"Process Strategy":

Use these strategies to stretch those with potential without major risk. Many of the concepts can be pitched on paper, reviewed, validated, and approved before physical action is taken. Talent development is key within supply chain so do not underestimate processes that can enable this strategy.

VENDOR MANAGED INVENTORY (VMI)

A similar concept to SOMI is vendor managed inventory (VMI) it differs in the fact that the consuming company owns the inventory but the vendor manages it either onsite or at their facility. This has two main benefits in the business environment. First is when a company subcontracts a process out to a supplier. Here the supplier can add value without carrying the expense of the inventory. The consuming company can maintain control of the inventory and the inventory levels also. In addition the consuming business can also use their buying power to negotiate lower procurement costs. Second, a consuming company can hire a vendor to manage inventory at their location. This can leverage vendor expertise and efficiencies to reduce cost and mismanagement at a consuming company location, yet maintain the inventory in a readily available location.

The advantages of implementing VMI are many but the primary advantages are the use of the subcontractor's ability or capacity without loss of inventory control. In addition they can maintain the leverage of the larger company's cash flow, buying power, and planning resources. VMI also reduces the need for financial exchange and in some cases it can reduce taxes and tariffs. Use of VMI can also increase the flexibility and agility through the use of multiple sources to cover capacity constraints and reduce risks related to sole sourcing or other business continuity risks.

"Quick win" projects:

1. If not completed in a SOMI exercise, compile a list of as many suppliers as possible. Organize and rank them on three criteria; size of supplier's total business, annual sales to company, and trustworthiness. For VMI, the trustworthiness is gauged more on planning and execution capabilities and less on financial trustworthiness. In turn this means that some suppliers may not have been SOMI eligible but could be VMI candidates. As before, this should not be an exact science but do not ignore accuracy. Some companies have robust versions of this already, if so then look to refresh and supplement where needed.

   Grading the supplier's total size of business relative to the other suppliers by use of scale of high, medium, low, or 1-10 will be sufficient. The annual spend the company makes on the supplier should be available from procurement or finance. Leave the measurement in financial terms and in this case it should be fairly accurate but does not have to be exact. A supplemental measurement that shows the percentage of spend vs. the total supply spend will also be handy. Last is trustworthiness. It is likely there will be a need to start with instinctive scoring. Try to make it more scientific and less emotive. Remember in this case to focus on execution reliability and not on the financials. Look to planners and procurement to integrate supplier assessments, risk of origin, government impacts, and physical location into the analysis.

Theoretical return: A pivotal item that if clear and available will be used widely in supply chain decisions and strategies. Information will show benefit in the hands of logistics, procurement, planning, Operational Excellence, and of course inventory teams.

2. Use the compilation of supplier information to start a "what if" conversation with key partners. Now look to invite more operational team members that show ability to grind through yet with sparks if innovative first inceptor passion. This team can be more centered in procurement and supply chain, warehousing, and inventory. This is a scoping conversation; no action should take place until the exercise is complete. Intent is for the team to develop a supplier ranking measures the fit of a supplier in a VMI environment. There is no correct answer, if the ranking does not work then go back and try a different ranking approach.

   A likely VMI candidate should be agile and willing to make adjustments, have robust planning and management capabilities, and be able to add value and product expertise either through onsite or offsite management of inventories. Compile a list of the top candidates for VMI conversations and start to socialize with a broader leadership but be sure to socialize the risks along with the benefits.

   Theoretical return: Building the concept of working outside the company's walls will provide great gains in maturity. The value is not only in building a VMI list but building a rigor and understanding of suppliers, many other ideas or actions may blossom for the momentum created here.

3. Take the newly created list of VMI candidates and look to organize them by the mutual benefits. Look for the supplier that would add the greatest incremental benefit and work with the appropriate teams to see if they feel they can leverage this as a negotiation or what costs may come with it. Validate this information and then compare it to the expected gains. If there is a net benefit, look to put together a project to implement on a small number of suppliers as a pilot. Monitor the relationship until it is clear to the benefits and any unintended consequences are revealed before expanding to additional vendors.

    Theoretical return: This pre-work and pilot will ensure the proper actions success when scaling the concept of VMI. Expect lessons to be learned and plan to collaborate with the supplier providing gives and takes where needed. For greatest benefit and return provide ample training and time to initiate the pilot and study its lessons.

"Quick Win" Predecessors: Concepts of pooling and initial pre-work for SOMI and VMI should be completed before a pilot for either is ran. Strong education plans will also be important for success.

"Game Changer" project:

Look to expand and leverage VMI only where the right fit exists, although VMI may have a broader capacity than SOMI and may be easier to implement in many industries. Expand the pilot concept to all suppliers where it provides the right value. An over expansion or premature set up has proven to be very costly. A well balanced management of suppliers through the use of standard supply relationships, pooling, SOMI, and VMI will result a highly effective model.

> *"Game Changer" predecessors: A stable pilot program that can clearly articulate the gains while identify and address unintended consequences.*

Continuous Improvement Environment:

Review VMI relationships every few years or at contract renewals. If set up correctly, this process of a supplier review and ranking becomes a highly impactful document. It will show such a value that it will naturally grow support and sustainability across the company. In many cases it will find a natural fit and ownership will become cross functional with many departments looking to support the inventory strategy.

Culture: Collaborative and Rigorous

"Process Strategy":

Use these strategies to stretch those with potential without major risk. Assign up and coming talent to lead these activities. Many of the concepts can be pitched on paper, reviewed, validated, and approved before physical action is taken. This will help mitigate the risk of error from developing talent yet stretch and grow their abilities quickly with highly visible and impactful projects. Talent development is essential within supply chain so do not underestimate processes that can provide such development and strategy.

DELAYED DIFFERENTIATION

Delayed Differentiation (DD) is a single pooling strategy that is often considered because it covers many (but not all) of the optimization considerations that come with pooling strategy. This policy attempts to delay the decision of differentiation, or a final change, in the product for as long as possible but does not come without incremental planning or costs. Most often it requires a more complex supply chain or BOM that integrates a "naked" form of a finished good or intermediate step between two steps in a BOM. This strategy is not for low maturity supply chains. Its feasibility and expected outcomes should be in line with the current maturity assessment. A company track record of successful implementations with in the simpler pooling strategies should be a strong indicator of business readiness for delayed differentiation.

Imagine three customers all buy the exact same product but all require a different printing on the box. To respond, the supplier no longer packages directly into a final box. Rather the company completes the full assembly and packaging with a blank box and ships these blank boxes to the warehouse. Now the warehouse adds an additional step to finalize the packaging by putting on an outer box with all the printed marketing just before it ships. The location of differentiation changed. The process changed by adding a step. In exchange for the added costs, the inventory is pooled in a more flexible presentation and they can react to orders faster, thus adding more overall value than cost.

"Quick win" projects:

1. Compile a view of demand variability for each SKU-location across the supply chain. If base capabilities and systems are not in place to do so, focus on a couple top brands. Identify node families where the greatest amount of pooling would exist by this process. Note that the greatest opportunity for pooling may not be the sources with the greatest variability as pooling of demand and variability requires an offsetting variability. For example when one market over forecasts, another market in the same family under forecasts.

   Theoretical return: This step is necessary to learn and set up a proof of value for the concept. While return may not be immediate, it is a critical exploratory step that should be completed before the concept is discussed as a strategy.

2. Also compile a list of physical attributes of these products including region, supplying plant, and storage warehouse of the product. Identify the families that would benefit from offsetting variability, reside in the same warehouse (or neighboring warehouses), and are in the same sales region. This is a list that could be considered for delayed differentiation. Compile a list of the potential gains and costs and socialize the value proposition. If the value proposition is not strong enough, consider those families for postponement or deferment.

   Theoretical return: This step is necessary for the project. While return may not be immediate, it is a critical exploratory step that should be completed before the concept is discussed as a strategy.

3. Take one or two of the highest impact cases for DD and explore the concept. Compile a core team to put together a more robust, yet theoretical, process and to run a Proof of Concept. Incorporate algorithms and metrics that can reenact the value that would have resulted over the last year if the newly formed DD concept would have been in place. Ensure robustness by running a few scenarios that either are likely to happen and impact results, or nearly happened with this or a similar product in the last year. Share the results and if no major feasibility concerns arise work with the core team to do a live implementation of a single DD process.

   Theoretical return: Delayed Differentiation will have a mix of lessons learned so ROI of the first implementation may be mixed also. Do not give up but be aware that this is not a one size fits all model and the law of diminishing returns will likely take place here.

4. Once the first implementation is stabilized, revisit the priority list. Refresh the data and assumptions. Additionally, add in the benefit of the newly enhanced supply chain where DD was implemented into the prioritization. Reduced costs and efforts will add benefit to products in the same environment affecting the same team members and likely drive a faster return. The second implementation in the same location may also provide incremental value and enhancements to the first process implemented.

   Theoretical return: The second and third implementations will likely add the most value. If not, revisit assumptions or consider the strategy. In this case maybe a postponement or deferment strategy, or maybe even a SOMI or VMI capacity may drive better value.

"Quick Win" Predecessors: Delayed differentiation is a higher level maturity concept and thus should be respected as such. Ensure the supply chain is properly equipped and capable of handling the process. If not, and aspirations remain, consider deferment or possibly postponement.

"Game Changer" project:

Integrate a hybrid model with specific attributes and criteria that slots future products into different levels of candidacy. Some or all of the simpler policies deferment, postponement, VMI, and SOMI, should now have foundational implementations. Combining all of the implemented policies and providing directional insight to when, where, and how to implement these strategies to new products will create a strategic advantage that very few companies can claim.

"Game Changer" predecessors: Implementation and strong foundations of a few of the inventory process management strategies.

Continuous Improvement Environment:

The supply chain remains ever changing which means the analysis and review of candidacy should not stop. If specific attributes and criteria were properly defined the analytic review should not be too difficult or time consuming. Provide visibility and measurements to products that are implemented and those that remain candidates. In addition ensure the value metrics and KPIs are in place showing the perpetual savings being accumulated through the additional efforts.

Culture: Dynamic Leadership and Persistent

"Process Strategy":

This is a large risk-reward strategy so ensure the strategy is robust and the leadership is dynamic in a way that they can adjust to change.   Be persistent to drive completion and excellence as this is not an easy or cheap solution.   Drive strategic growth through highlighting opportunities visible in the measurements and metrics implemented with the DD policies.

MANUFACTURING POSTPONEMENT

Manufacturing Postponement can often be mistaken for DD and vice versa. This type of postponement is a broader and simpler tactic that can often come with alternative benefits. It can also attain a portion of DD benefits without the cost of an intermediary.   A manufacturing postponement strategy postpones a standard process to a location further downstream closer to customer (ex. Package at a warehouse instead of plant with no change in SKUs or process, just location). This puts the decision closer to the customer and enables the manufacturing and supply chain team to customize and finalize faster and in a more agile way.

Imagine the same scenario as before where three customers require three different packages. Instead of creating additional steps and costs, now the supplier just finalizes the packaging by assembling and packaging the goods into the box at the warehouse instead of upstream at the production site, using the same process the production site would have used. Now the finalization can be completed closer to the need and specific to an order rather than to forecast upstream. As a result the inventory is held as more flexible components and the decision to finalize is postponed to a later point where a more accurate decision can be made. Often this requires investment in equipment and training at the warehouse but usually provides a process with higher agility to package more exact amounts with shorter lead times.

"Quick win" projects:

1. Start with finished goods and compile a view of forecast changes and forecast error for each customer facing SKU-location on a time lagged basis. This can be done in conjunction with postponement exercise. Identify the forecast error at one time increment out from delivery, two time increments, three time increments, and so forth until the timeframe that provides full flexibility in supply. Compile a similar list of changes in forecast between time periods. List and rank SKUs by those that have the greatest improvement from one time increment to another, and create another list of SKUs that have the greatest overall improvement.

   Theoretical return: This step is necessary for the project. While return may not be immediate, it is a critical exploratory step that should be completed before the concept is discussed as a strategy.

2. Take one or two of the highest impact cases and explore the concept of postponing a change in the product to a downstream location in an attempt to get this decision closer to the customer. In addition to being the top of the list, the product also has to meet the criteria that there is an opportunity to customize at a later point downstream. This will entail either the addition of another location or a likely customization if there is a downstream location. If a SKU meets all criteria and there is alignment on the concept look to assemble a core team and implement a small family of SKUs as a beta.

   Theoretical return: Postponement will have some complexity and likely have costs connected to the learning. Postponement ultimately can have strong return, not only direct from the financial project ROI but through increased customer service and opportunity for agility and customization to meet customer needs.

3. Once the first implementation is stabilized revisit the priority list. Refresh the data and assumptions. Additionally add in the benefit of the newly enhanced supply chain postponement capabilities that now exist into the prioritization. Reduced costs and efforts will add benefit to products in the same environment affecting the same team members and likely drive a faster return. The second implementation in the same location may also provide incremental efficiencies and value to the first process implemented.

   Theoretical return: The second and third implementations will likely add the most value. If not, revisit assumptions or consider the strategy. In the case return continues to decline, maybe a deferment or VMI strategy may work better.

"Quick Win" Predecessors: No predecessors are required to scope the idea but doing the proper due diligence and maturity assessment will add immense value in the implementation of a postponement strategy. Also, consider the simpler deferment strategy first as in many cases it comes with less cost and can have equally strong benefit.

"Game Changer" project:

Explore the concept of putting postponement capabilities at all customer facing warehouses. Implementing this capability as a single project may incorporate many cost and time efficiencies. While more difficult to analyze expand the review upstream to additional echelons in the supply chain and look for easy value where equipment and expertise already exist in a downstream manufacturing location. Be aware that this is a much more difficult step to accurately compile variability information in many businesses.

"Game Changer" predecessors: A proven capability and strong ROI on prior implemented postponement strategies.

Continuous Improvement Environment:

If at first there is no success, give it time and analyze again. Do not let postponement become a forbidden word. It works well when implemented in the proper environment. If the business environment is better suited for other pooling strategies, then focus the time and continuous improvement on those strategies but as the supply chain environment changes do not be afraid to review the strategies again.

Culture: Six Sigma and Consumer Focused

"Process Strategy":

Postponement does not come without expense. Be sure that the manufacturing and supply chain can support it properly. Do a preparedness assessment on the capabilities of both people and technology and do a risk assessment on process. If these are overlooked and postponement results in customer service or quality issues, it will be painful to remediate.

DEFERMENT

Deferment is the act of putting something off to a later time. Note that this definition does not involve a different place or product, just time. Sometimes simple is best, deferment can create great advantages when the risk of the unknown is the highest. It is natural to defer when unknown so sometimes it is ok not to fight it. An alternative postponement could be to wait closer to customer demand to take action (example ship more frequently from a primary warehouse to a DC or distributor in an attempt to prevent over shipment and redeployment).

Imagine the same scenario as before where three customers require three different packages. Instead of creating additional steps and costs, now the supplier now just waits to finalize the production time and quantity until closer to the customer need. As a result, the inventory is held as more flexible components and the decision to finalize is postponed to a later time when a more accurate decision can be made.

"Quick win" projects:

1. Start with finished goods and compile a view of forecast changes and forecast error for each customer facing SKU-location on a time lagged basis. This can be done in conjunction with a postponement exercise. Identify the forecast error at one time increment out from delivery, two time increments, three time increments, and so forth until the timeframe that provides full flexibility in supply is identified. Compile a similar list of changes in forecast between time periods. List and rank SKUs by those that have the greatest improvement from one time increment to another, and create another list of SKUs that have the greatest overall improvement.

    Theoretical return: This step is necessary for the project. While return may not be immediate, it is a critical exploratory step that should be completed before the concept is discussed as a strategy.

2. Take one or two of the highest impact cases and explore the concept of deferring a decision to change the product to a later time in order to attain a more accurate signal or plan. If a SKU meets this simple criteria and there is alignment on the concept look to assemble a core team and implement a small family of SKUs as a proof of concept.

    Theoretical return: Deferment is the least expensive and complex of the pooling strategies to implement so it can often have strong returns very quickly.

3. Once the first implementation is stabilized revisit the priority list. Refresh the data and assumptions. Additionally add in the benefit of the newly enhanced supply chain

deferment capabilities, focusing on educated and mature area, and add this into the consideration where reviewing SKUs with the highest potential. Costs may not decrease with each incremental implementation.

Theoretical return: Costs may not decrease dramatically with each incremental addition of deferment. It may be likely to see diminishing returns after a certain point but ROI may remain high as expenses would stay low. Return can be increased by grouping multiple SKUs into future implementations at the same location.

"Quick Win" Predecessors: No predecessors are required and due to the flexibility and simplicity deferment is often the easiest of the pooling strategies to start with. It is highly encouraged to match the project strategy with the current maturity of the areas being addressed. Consider a maturity assessment in the initial stages of scoping.

"Game Changer" project:

Develop automated and robust planning software and policies that enable "automatic" deferment decisions. These decisions should still be audited by planner initially but eventually be moved to an exception audit basis. This requires dynamic production windows or broader flexibility to defer within frozen windows of production.

"Game Changer" predecessors: This project should be developed off from the process and lessons compiled from implementing deferment manually. A foundational deferment process should be in self-sustaining before consideration of an automated system.

Continuous Improvement Environment:

Develop a desire to be more agile and react closer to customer needs. Look to integrate simple decisions with high impact and low rework. These strategies for continuous improvement related to deferment will most easily be accomplished through education and understanding.

Culture: Flexible and Responsive

"Process Strategy":

The strategy of deferment is to reduce waste by making a decision closer to the time of customer demand. This improves the planning and production accuracy, reduces the efforts related to rework or adjustments, and reduces inventory and production ineffectiveness. Ultimately it will save time and frustration. If this value and effectiveness is clear to the team members they will drive their own passion to improve through smarter decisions closer to the customer demand.

PATTERNED PRODUCTION PLANNING & OPTIMIZATION (PPPO)

The use of inventory planning to drive production efficiencies is not a new idea but, until the era of true big data scenario capabilities, was nearly impossible to effectively achieve due to the multi-echelon layers of complexity and inter-dependencies. It usually requires maturity in planning but if done properly even a planning process with low maturity can successfully take steps towards patterning and gain robust benefits.   Concepts of production wheels can work in conjunction with PPPO but are a separate concept.

This strategy will effectively and efficiently reduce or remove changeovers and down time between certain production runs. It organizes upstream planning through the use of optimization techniques to reduce the overall downtime, number of changeovers, and resulting inventories based on optimal time and value, post constraints. It can also reduce downstream risks and impacts as the added agility provided by the optimization is able to absorb some of the change requests and upstream delay.

"Quick win" projects:

1. Identify the basic production flow down to the level of production lines, subassembly locations, and storage locations along with each of their total capacities. Look and compare redundancies that exist such as multiple subassembly locations that could possibly accept a given production order if equipped properly. Do this to raise awareness of all the theoretical options. Raise awareness but be clear that this is not intended to question the current planning footprint or prior decisions and strategies. Rather this awareness is to develop the proper due diligence and scope.

   Theoretical return: Do not take this lightly and do the proper research. Investment in talent and technology will be heavy to deliver effective returns. Research is cheap, do not be afraid to get your feet wet, even if it is not the right fit - the knowledge and understanding gained will be worth the time spent.

2. Gather a cross-functional core team into a room and walk through the concept of a single production pattern within a subassembly group. Keep the change management hat on and be sure to invite future key stakeholders that will need to align and understand. Try to get operational excellence or a neutral team experienced with driving change to facilitate. Have as much homework prepared as possible to increase learning and success.

   Theoretical return: Even if PPPO does make it to implementation the Kaizen (improvement) style learning event will add new visibility, opportunity, and passion for some of the team members. Continue to work with these individuals as the will help drive future improvements in production.

3. Implementation will take sustainability. Before implementation starts look to align and educate the teams. Confirm the proper sustainability of staffing and resourcing before project kickoff. Kick off the project by scoping and defining the business requirements to implement a basic improvement to planning. This could be as simple as an enhancement in a spreadsheet or basic production planning software. Rapidly follow this up with another and another. Intent is to build the maturity and flush out any data issues. Do this before consideration of make or buy of a sophisticated system.

   Theoretical return: This investment will not go to waste. Even simple enhancements to current programs can bring great value. It also helps the team understand and make a more educated decision when picking a software company.

"Quick Win" Predecessors: No predecessors are required but commitment to provide sufficient resources is a must. In addition the programs have to be targeted for the proper maturity level. Since this type of data is not commonly necessary there is potential to have need for heavy amounts of data remediation or development.

"Game Changer" project:

Assess the potential software solutions in a make vs. buy scenario. Compare options and capabilities in the current maturity state and the end maturity state. Confirm that each option can support both scenarios. Also consider the timeframe of implementation and the opportunity costs. Large investments such as this come with the need of timely return so be prepared to deliver on time in full before committing to spend. The potential for return can give a true competitive advantage as it will utilize downtime and increase agility in the manufacturing area and the perpetual expense to do so are quite low versus the return. In the right environment this may result in the avoidance of additional lines or facilities, loss of sales or market share due to capacity constraints, and overall reduction of fixed expense allocation per unit impacting cost of goods sold (COGS).

"Game Changer" predecessors: All early stages and data remediation should be completed. Alignment across GMS should be in place. Proper funding and long term resources should be available.

Continuous Improvement Environment:

Look to provide a progressive improvement to production efficiency with a continuous "natural" reduction of inventory between nodes. Look to integrate simple changes that have impactful results. Encourage planners to challenge the process. Build relationships with teams on the production lines and look to share their ideas and expertise. Proper mentorship and training for planners to make certain proper efficiencies are realized is an absolute must for success.

Culture: Efficient and Progressive

"Process Strategy":

Commitment to provide sufficient resources is a must. In addition, the programs have to be targeted for the proper maturity level. Since the type of data necessary is not commonly used elsewhere there is potential to have a need for heavy amounts of data remediation or development. Start small and build but keep pushing to add momentum.

PRODUCTION WHEELS

Production Wheels have their place and work well in many environments and fail miserably in others. They must be managed effectively and must have the right production attributes to be successful. If one or the other is missing the concept is unlikely to succeed. A production wheel is a concept of planning inventory and production in such a cadence that no matter what the demand the same cadence will be followed for a set period of time, at which time new parameters will be set to rebalance, and then the process is repeated again. While similar to a rhythm wheel they have a clear difference in attributes and approach.

"Quick win" projects:

1. Planning maturity is essential in the development of a production wheel. Take the first level as an opportunity to explore and improve current production planning and demand planning. Gather the planning teams together and hold a continuous improvement event to identify gaps, process improvements, and to map out the "as is" process. Consider not telling the team the intent of exploring a production wheel yet, it may change the way in which they participate and outcome of the event. Drive visibility, understanding, and education through the event and through one on one follow ups with each team member.

   Theoretical return: With exploration as the "hidden" but primary reason, these events often drive other added value in planning improvements in addition to the underlying agenda.

2. Synthesize all the new data and compare the current capabilities to those necessary to drive production wheel planning. Teams need to be able to accurately lock in production for extended time periods so that there is stability in the production wheel. In addition upstream and downstream planning needs to be able to support this. Considerations should include proper upstream production capacity and absorption of possible idle capacity upstream, and confirmation of sufficient storage capacity downstream. If forecast variability or forecast error variability is high a production wheel may not drive the most value. If all

possible concerns are removed or mitigated and a production wheel is deemed viable and adds value then gather a core team to explore further.

Theoretical return: Production Wheels take a lot of work and planning and can be very costly if implemented incorrectly. Take time to ensure accurate results, time spent here will pay dividends on future steps.

3. Implementation will take sustainability. Before implementation starts look to align and educate the teams. Confirm the proper education and sustainability of staffing and resourcing before implementation kickoff. Scoping should be complete and countermeasures in place for potential risks. Once developed and tested, run planning software in parallel to production for a few cycles. Do not get too comfortable too quickly, as small imbalances will grow over time. It will be easy to get impatient and want return on the investment sooner but be diligent. If implemented before all the bugs are worked out it can be very costly to fix and will likely result in customer service failures before it can be corrected.

Theoretical return: Given the right environment production wheels have immense savings in production. Be careful not to offset gains by driving too many incremental costs elsewhere.

"Quick Win" Predecessors: Production wheels must have the proper environment to work well. Strong gains from primary line efficiencies, planning efficiencies, and low impact due to holding costs and forecast error are needed. Stable production planning with reasonably high maturity and depth are also necessary.

"Game Changer" project:

Implement a production wheel that balances upstream production and downstream inventory. Consider this capacity at major points throughout manufacturing and not just close to finished goods. Through managing a single point or "lever" there is potential to drive a balanced and highly efficient production cycle with little to no downtime or customer impact.

"Game Changer" predecessors: An effective and sustainable production wheel in the fulcrum of the analysis.

Continuous Improvement Environment:

Integrating an anticipatory mindset with the proper measurements will be critical. Teams have to be able to foresee and make a change over time. This is like driving a big ship with a very small rudder, either they have to commit early and react slowly or the need a tug boat (countermeasure) to help enact a large course correction. Changing direction regularly in a "wheel" environment will come at great costs.

Culture: Anticipatory and Controlled

"Process Strategy":

Think strategically on where, when, and why to implement a production wheel. Consider more locations than just those closest to finished goods (agility close to customer, efficiency close to supplier). Be diligent in the pre-work, once a production wheel is live lessons become expensive. Know the risks and unintended consequences. Insist in countermeasures and ways to adjust if necessary. Stay close and do not lose sight of process, check in regularly once implemented. Mentor and lead the planning team and ensure proper education, training, and support outlets.

LEAPFROGGING

Faster is not always better. Stepping back and understanding the full picture and use of inventory within the supply chain can reap benefits in parallel areas without incremental costs to inventory. This may add net financial benefit, but even if a small net expense exists originally it is still well worth it. Leapfrogging is an example of this where the concept of slowing down logistics (ocean instead of air, or train instead of truck) enables a supply chain countermeasure that did not exist before. With the concept of Leapfrogging the supply chain, by slowing down the logistics leg and taking advantage of savings, can now leap over a missed shipment and expedite one of the following shipments without impact to the downstream customer. This saves logistics expense but more importantly it reduces variability within supply chain, thus improving customer service and reducing safety stock. In addition the increased pipeline (logistics) stock may not be all incremental as there may be opportunity to use and redeploy inventory held downstream of a bottleneck. The extra pipeline stock created by implementing Leapfrogging can help meet the buffer requirements that are necessary downstream of a bottleneck.

"Quick win" projects:

1. Gather and analyze the logistics expedite expenses and a list of item locations that did not meet customer service level targets. Work with logistics to identify potential of using leapfrogging to improve customer service and reduce expedite and general logistics expenses. This can be done on a subset or all opportunities based on resources to do so. Target the use of a slower logistics mode in order to add the capability to recover from upstream supply delays. By utilizing the faster mode on the same lane when delays occur it will improve customer service and reduce impact on downstream production. In this case inventory is used strategically and may experience an overall increase, although inventory costs need to be weighed into the overall value of the strategy. Keep in mind to include an estimated savings for reduced safety stock downstream as variability risks should be decreased through the leapfrogging strategy.

   If the analysis shows potential opportunity and the value proposition is strong, socialize the concept with supply chain leaders to look for sponsorship. Once sponsored and approved, then look to compile a core team to include logistics leads and experts along with inventory experts. Usually, it will be best to implement all products for a lane at once, so efficient loads can be maintained. Consider one lane to begin with in order to limit the impact of mistakes and lessons learned then expand as maturity develops.

   Theoretical return: Be clear that initially costs may go up but customer service and less tangible savings such as reduced variability, downtime, and changeover downstream will add to the savings or cost avoidance. Over time, downstream safety stocks and other buffers should decrease as supply variability should reduce upstream.

2. Compile a list of logistics modes by each shipment lane and product. If possible, also add in the financial spend per lane. If not possible, incorporate an estimated financial spend per lane. Work with logistics to further compile a list of lanes and potential to reduce costs by changing mode of transportation. Provide an estimated percent savings from current by each mode and lane by comparing current spot quotes between both modes. The logistics team should be able to help provide this information.

    Multiply this savings by the current lane cost for the past year of shipments and rank lanes by this rough estimate of potential savings. Then compare the increased days of transit times the cost of an average day of inventory for that lane. Multiply this increased inventory cost times the higher of the holding cost of inventory or the opportunity cost of capital. Develop a new list ranked by savings resulting from comparing the reduced logistics expenses by the new transit mode minus the additional cost of carrying additional inventory. If opportunity remains, gather a cross functional team, including a sponsoring leader, to explore feasibility and impactions of a handful of lanes.

    Theoretical return: Return not only comes in the identified savings from the project but also the increased customer service by enabling this strategy.

3. Consider a leapfrogging strategy primarily for logistics savings. This will be most successful where downstream

cycle or safety stocks are quite large. Usually these large safety stocks are for reasons such as upstream bottlenecks or risk mitigation from risks related to a single source upstream. Make certain that the change in logistic strategy from leapfrogging is downstream of the related constraint. It will also be best served if more inventories are effectively removed downstream to offset the extra inventory needed to implement the leapfrogging strategy.

> *Theoretical return: Usually this has a strong ROI with little to no change to inventory costs and considerable savings in logistics costs.*

"Quick Win" Predecessors: A stable and understood logistics and inventory network are necessary to implement leapfrogging. A clear understanding of tradeoffs and the ability to estimate savings will be necessary.

"Game Changer" project:

Consider a multi-mode network balancing three or more modes in a given transportation lane. Implementation is similar to a dual mode tradeoff but takes a higher degree of expertise and rigor as now there are multiple combinations of options to consider for each decision. Strong decision matrices and training programs will be necessary in most cases to ensure teams are implementing the best combination of policies. These requirements may change as logistic costs and inventory requirements constantly change. As a result, ensure regular tracking of the process and value along with regular analysis of optimal combinations and updated matrices.

The most difficult consideration may be how to balance multiple lead time requirements in planning to assure the necessary planning. If not able to vary this lead time and attain timely decisions, consider use of the longest transit time for lead times. This basically will result in two or more choices to meet expedite needs. There can still be great value in doing so but ensure there is enough inventories to move upstream to compensate for the additional pipeline stock required.

> *"Game Changer" predecessors: An effective standard leapfrogging strategy should be implemented before adding the additional risks and complexities of a multi-mode network of leapfrogging.*

Continuous Improvement Environment:

Leapfrogging lends well to a strong focus on total landed costs of inventory. Leverage this by providing visible impacts and values through metrics and training. There likely will be a strong push back from those that show concern for increased inventory. Odds are these stakeholders do not understand the tradeoffs of inventory and logistics nor do they have concern that their accountabilities are being negatively impacted.

Culture: Prudent and Agile

"Process Strategy":

Leapfrogging may seem like a fairly simple process to implement but do not underestimate the change management necessary to implement. Drive a strategy that educates on the value of focusing on total landed costs. Enable ways to break down barriers and prevent negatively affecting accountabilities of other stakeholders. This likely will require alignment and understanding from Senior Leadership to adjust those accountabilities.

Drive a strategy that creates a total cost down structure. Focus the strategy in such a way that the core team looks to provide an optimal solution that is agile enough to react as needed with minimal additional expense. Do not let inventory revert back and become imbalanced or offset the gains from the leapfrogging efforts. Assure that all aspects of leapfrogging are implemented together. For example do not let the inventory remain once the logistics change has been implemented and stabilized. Keep focus on the overall value and accountability by providing the proper visibility to metrics and savings.

OPERATIONAL EXCELLENCE

Operational Excellence is all about running a plant or supply chain efficiently through the use of programs such as LEAN and SIX SIGMA. Due to the tangible and understandable nature of these programs, they are the most common and focused programs but are not the only aspects that can drive Operational Excellence. This does not mean that they will have the highest ROIs or the most effective change.

Programs like this are often the simplest of the possibilities and rarely are entirely comprehensive in order to cover the most effective and optimized tradeoffs. In addition, the can regularly lack the accountability to ensure the change is sustained long term as many practitioners move from one project to another, hopping from bottleneck to bottleneck or from one long lead time to another. Some of the more refined practitioners will move focus from the highly visible issue to the root causes of these issues and incorporate more culture building techniques and change management tactics. These take much more time but address the maturity and sustainability of the process. In addition they will look to drive a multi-level improvement within their strategy.

A rebalance of inventory is the net result of a successful operational excellence strategy. The top practitioners understand their inventory well and use the success of inventory as a key indicator of the success of their program. Enable the development of operational excellence by providing a much needed and highly valued organization of support and optimization. The tools at hand for inventory strategies integrate well into operational excellence programs, just as operational excellence procedures and culture is used throughout successful inventory strategies.

"Quick win" projects:

1. Build a relationship operational excellence leadership and strong ties throughout the levels of the operational excellence teams. Share how operational excellence is important to the inventory strategy and how the inventory tools and metrics are symbiotic with operational excellence strategies. Discuss these synergies and look to support the operational excellence team in their goals. Do not ask for change yet, just introducing the inventory capabilities into these decisions is the key objective.

   Theoretical return: Introducing inventory tools and strategies to operational excellence will pay immediate and long term dividends with just a little extra effort to support the team. Be sure to staff appropriately to support the initiative.

2. Analyze the opportunities to collaborate with operational excellence. Compare metrics of both operational excellence and inventory. See where these metrics can be combined or used in both teams. Identify how these combined metrics can help drive improved decision for operational excellence. Look to identify areas of high variability or bottlenecks and share these opportunities with operational excellence. Collaborate together to identify the return and how to integrate these opportunities into the operational excellence portfolio.

    Theoretical return: As these issues get resolved through operational exercises, the positive inventory impact will be realized. By collaborating with the team and utilizing operational excellence tools the return on effort will have an exponential value.

3. Study the operational excellence projects being implemented. Learn what is being implemented and what results are expected. Provide support and additional commitments to ROIs by aligning inventory changes or strategies that will take advantage of the operational excellence improvements. Provide feedback to what could be done to gain this additional value and, if any, what tweaks or adjustments will be necessary to attain these results.

    Theoretical return: Collaborative projects often return the highest gains for both teams even if the individual project may not have been the top priority for that team.

"Quick Win" Predecessors: A robust understanding of inventory processes, metrics, and tools are necessary to provide the proper subject matter expertise and solutions.

"Game Changer" project:

Collaborate with Operational Excellence to identify new opportunities and ways to implement their projects. Use multiple inventory strategy tools and scenario planning to project the value of the improvements. Over time learn the operational excellence strategy to proactively identify opportunities and correlating return for operational excellence. This will help them build a stronger portfolio to discuss and build their strategy.

"Game Changer" predecessors: A strong collaboration with operational excellence and working understanding of their concept are a must. Consider implementing multiple projects together where inventory strategies provide valued support and incremental gains for operational excellence before trying to implement a more aggressive tactic such as this.

Continuous Improvement Environment:

This strategy comes with the true meaning of continuous improvement. Integration of accountability, sustainability, and educated decisions should be prevalent. Expect to challenge the status quo and drive maturity more quickly than with other teams. Do not underestimate the required change management to do so. Look to build relationships and be prepared to educate about inventory along the way. Once alignment is attained, the operational excellence team should be able to quickly understand and integrate inventory information and input into their processes.

Culture: Supportive and Continuous

"Process Strategy":

Learning and practicing the operational excellence concepts throughout the inventory strategies will provide additional gains in the projects and integrate the two departments. These departments should remain separate without dotted line reporting. Rather the two should act more like fraternal twins carrying many of the same traits and goals yet look, feel, and operate slightly different.

OPERATIONAL EXCELLENCE PORTFOLIO

The Op Ex portfolio is a complete list of all the projects in which the team has been asked to own or support. These projects are likely to have some of the highest sponsorship, broadest visibility, and most noticeable impact. This team has a high accountability and lots of pressure to deliver this portfolio.

The use of inventory management scenarios can be the most effective way for Op Ex to prioritize the impact of their projects. In order for the team to attain an accurate ROI of each project it takes considerable effort. The inventory management tools and scenario capabilities can integrate such changes and report out a before and after scenario along with the savings. Without it, project ROIs are usually estimated and commonly overstated versus the actual return attained. Integrating the inventory impacts into the Op Ex portfolio will help ensure the most effective prioritization and improve the accuracy of the results.

"Quick win" projects:

1. Provide Op Ex support by using the inventory scenario planning tools to provide before and after scenarios. Set up the scenario comparison and savings based on the current status of the supply chain and current guidance of Op Ex with proposed changes to isolate these from any other possible impacts. Do not initiate additional ideas or synergies at this point yet. Alignment and understanding of what has been completed is important at this stage. If done accurately and per their requirements, this should build strong trust and improved relationship with the Op Ex team.

   Theoretical return: The return comes from building the relationship and not showing off skills. Be careful to focus return on Op Ex projects and not on the inventory strategy.

2. Look for additional savings inside of the Op Ex Portfolio by using the inventory scenario tools to add in incremental inventory strategies that can drive additional value to the Op Ex projects. Once completed, reevaluate the total project savings and integrate the new savings into the portfolio prioritization. Socialize the opportunities with the Op Ex team and work to collaborate. Be prepared to allocate additional inventory resources to support the extra work necessary to attain the additional value.

   Theoretical return: Return will be high as long as the right subject matter resources are integrated into the project.

> *Expecting Op Ex to own and drive these additional initiatives without support will not likely result in success.*

> *"Quick Win" Predecessors: A robust understanding of inventory processes, metrics, and tools are necessary to provide the proper subject matter expertise and solutions. In addition an Op Ex background or ability to learn it quickly will improve results and the communication of the results. Building the relationship between the teams is as important as the results, thus build the relationship before showcasing results or trying to drive change.*

"Game Changer" project:

Consider reviewing the inventory strategy portfolio in conjunction with the Op Ex portfolio. By reviewing these two portfolios as if they were intra-dependent it will provide a truly optimized portfolio for both teams. Even greater value will come from this as when these two portfolios work together the amount of work and change management requirements decrease and they attain gains faster.

> *"Game Changer" predecessors: A strong collaboration with operational excellence and proven working relationship is necessary in order to attain. By proving the value of inventory scenario planning and strategies in the normal Op Ex prioritization, it will provide opportunity to implement this "game changer" strategy.*

Continuous Improvement Environment:

The Operational Excellence portfolio is the epitome of continuous improvement. Keep this at top of mind for all participants. The whole goal is to Kaizen, or to work together proactively to achieve regular, incremental improvements. This takes strong trust and relationships. Just like continuous improvement, these relationships need continuous focus and diligence.

Culture: Trust and Partnership

"Process Strategy":

This takes strong trust and relationships. Just like continuous improvement, these relationships need continuous focus and diligence. Take time to meet team members for lunch and to help them with their challenges. Showing them how the relationship is mutually beneficial and maintaining this trust and affiliation will be important to the overall success.

Look to drive continuous improvement through regular interaction. In addition to the relationship building also schedule time to collaborate. Schedule regular meetings to review portfolios and to team up on initiatives. Just like all relationships, this will take time and commitment so make sure the teams have allocated enough time to support each other.

SUPPLY CHAIN HEALTH

Supply chain health drives the success of a company. Whether directly, or indirectly, it is looked at heavily when pricing the stock. It helps attain incremental upside in sales, prevent downside from loss in customer service, and ultimately drives bottom line through efficient use of inventory and logistics through effective planning. The ability to efficiently plan, manage, and move inventory is the fundamental core to peak supply chain health.

"Quick win" projects:

1. Review the current reporting metrics and KPIs. Confirm if they are indicative of the health of the supply chain. Review the ability to proactively address issues and impact the success of the reports. Ensure the key talent is in place and up to speed on the needs of the business. Complete a "what if" exercise to see if the team could properly react to a severe impact to the supply chain. Whether it is a severe drop or increase in sales or a quick change in supply reliability or any other potential impact the team should be able to quickly countermeasure and mitigate much of the risk within the current cycle.

   Theoretical return: While only theoretical, great return can come from the efforts to ensure the supply chain is robust enough to maintain healthy working status even in times of major change.

2. Consider funding an external maturity assessment. Often internal views can overlook details or have bias to what may be good. An external entity that can benchmark the maturity of the overall business and assess the capabilities of the people, process, and technology will be a key consideration. Ensure this assessment is more than a simple interview process and that the external team triangulates multiple sources to assess each area of the supply chain. It is too easy for a single resource to provide a bias based what is best for them or what they think should be said.

Theoretical return: Return will be high as long as the right subject matter resources are integrated into the project. Expecting Op Ex to own and drive these additional initiatives without support will not likely result in success.

"Quick Win" Predecessors: No predecessors are necessary and while left for the end of the book it is likely a beginning step for many leaders.

"Game Changer" project:

Develop a mid to long term roadmap that is conducive to increasing the overall maturity of the complete end to end supply chain. This will likely result in some necessary actions from peers and partners outside of the formal supply chain organization. Review all the levels of maturity and incorporate as many projects and process as possible that will drive continuous improvement to the maturity of the total supply chain. Most often the lowest maturity is the weakest link so look to improve through a balanced maturity approach.

"Game Changer" predecessors: Consider readiness to drive such a change. Ensure the roadmap starts at a level that addresses the current maturities and implements the proper measurements early in the process. Also consider the change management needs of such a paradigm shift and address appropriately.

Continuous Improvement Environment:

Slow but steady wins this race, but aspire to go as quickly as possible as time is money. Sustainability will be key, keep the pace and roadmap aligned with the people, process, and technological capabilities. Build solid foundations and pressure test them before moving on to the next level of maturity strategies.

Culture: Big Picture and Shared

"Process Strategy":

While many concepts were outlined in this book, do not limit opportunities to just these. Rather use these concepts as catalysts for the teams to create a customized approach and plan that meets the needs of the business and that will drive the greatest change and to development. Start by understanding the status quo of inventory and know how to influence and measure the change. Define what success looks like and address maturity needs properly. By balancing maturity and defining success it will allow for the ability to simplify and course correct. Leverage inventory spend strategically and develop the paradigm shift to create a strategic advantage. By properly laying out a health assessment and customizing a plan to fit these strategies can catapult the business well ahead of its competition.

In Recap

If done without clear and concise strategy and realistic expectations there is enough here to paralyze any company, no matter how great. Be clear to the goals and how they lay the path to success. Do not expect 100% buy in but do drive for clear understanding and alignment to the end goals. Ensure the targets and projects are in line with the maturity of the company and that those accountable have a clear path to reach aspired levels and to increase the maturity of their pieces. Match the outlined strategies (and others) with the biggest gaps found in the company, then build on the maturity of the area. Remember that *enterprise inventory optimization* is a process of continuous improvement across all inventory. This should drive true best in class advantages across all of manufacturing and supply chain.

Finally, take advantage of these processes to develop a sustainable knowledge base and workforce that can support these new and more complex strategies and mentor them heavily but empower them to lead the next generation of supply chain. Incubation of talent that is able to take on future complexities will be pivotal for sustained success. Challenge these teams to work together to consistently do better and do not let roadblocks or mediocracy hold them back. If approaching a dead end find avenues to define new roads. Whether or not these new roads are small detours within the same process or they are entirely new projects with the same end goal, give motivated teams a means to success and they will succeed.

The success of the company relies on the development and growth of its people and processes. Diversity is more than race or religion diversity also comes in age, passion, and work experience. Do not overlook talent in any form or fashion or title. Make it less about the past resume and more about the empowerment and opportunity to truly succeed. Do not neglect key talent through the lack of proper recognition and title as this will come at a cost of the success of the program. Take a leap and enable, empower, and enrich by providing mentorship and opportunity. Remember with a little risk and strategy come great reward. *The greatest of leaders are remembered for what they enabled more so than for what they did.*